S omeone can conquer kingdoms and countries without being a hero; someone else can prove himself a hero by controlling his temper. Someone can display courage by doing the out-of-the-ordinary, another by doing the ordinary. The question is always: How does he do it?"

—SØREN KIERKEGAARD,
EITHER/OR PART II

TO ALL THOSE
WHO ADD LIGHT
AND LOVE TO
THE WORLD.

– C. M.

BUSHEL
& PECK
BOOKS

Text copyright © 2019 by Christy Monson

Illustrations copyright © 2019 by Kathrin Honesta, 11, 25; Lidia Tomashevskaya, 13, 61; Emma Allsup, 15, 29; Edith Kurosaka, 17, 53, 99; Wiliam Luong, 19, 27, 35, 37, 41, 51, 55, 57, 59, 63, 65, 69, 71, 73, 75, 77, 85, 87, 89, 95, 97, 103, 105, 107, 109; Chorkung Kung, 21, 91; Sabrina Gennari, 23; Vanya Firdausya, 31, 39, 79, 83; Luciagzz, 33, 101; Olja Maltzewa, 43; Spurga, 45; Herosuofficial, 47, 67; Victoria, 49; Robert Miles, 81; and Ermir, 93; respectively.

Published by Bushel & Peck Books, www.bushelandpeckbooks.com.

Some graphic elements licensed from Shutterstock artists, including Dastagir, Kovalto1, Puckung, Black Creator, M-O Vector, Artizarus, Rashad Ashur, Mr.Creative, Bearsky23, Trueffelpix, Dshnrgc, Popicon, Popcic, Vector Icon Flat, AF Studio, Bay_Design, Supanut Piyakanont, StockAppeal, BARS Graphics, VoodooDot, Kasue, Mikhail Grachikov, and Pensiri.

Bushel & Peck Books is dedicated to fighting illiteracy all over the world. For every book we sell, we donate one to a child in need—book for book. To nominate a school or organization to receive free books, please visit www.bushelandpeckbooks.com.

ISBN: 9781733633505

First Edition

Printed in China

10 9 8 7 6 5 4 3 2

50

Real

HEROES
FOR
BYS

TRUE STORIES OF COURAGE, INTEGRITY,
COMPASSION, LEADERSHIP, AND MORE!

by Christy Monson

CONTENTS

NOTE TO READER

Welcome to this extraordinary book of heroes! Here, you will find fifty incredible men and women from different times, places, and walks of life. Each is a real hero.

What makes a hero? Within these pages, you're about to find out. Sometimes, a hero is the person who fights bravely in the heat of battle. And sometimes, a hero is the person who knows when not to fight. Some heroes may seem larger than life. Others may seem small, quiet, even unimportant. But trust us, dear reader—their deeds have reverberated across the centuries.

There are many traits that can make someone a hero. Perhaps you've heard of superheroes who can fly or become invisible. In this book, you'll find twenty traits more powerful than even those—so powerful, in fact, that they have changed the course of history. We call each of these a "Special Power." They include the following:

- COMPASSION
- CONFIDENCE
- COURAGE
- CREATIVITY
- CURIOSITY
- EDUCATION
- FAMILY

- FITNESS
- FORGIVENESS
- FRIENDSHIP
- HARD WORK
- HUMOR
- INDEPENDENCE
- INTEGRITY

- INTELLIGENCE
- JUSTICE
- LEADERSHIP
- PATIENCE
- PERSEVERANCE
- SACRIFICE

After each story, you will find ideas for becoming a real hero yourself in a box labeled "You Can Be a Hero." Try the ideas and watch as you, too, start to make a positive difference in the world.

Now for a quick word about the people you will find in this book. In selecting these heroes, we have made an effort to choose people of integrity who tried to live heroically in all parts of their lives as spouses, parents, and neighbors. A faith leader once said, "The most important . . . work that you will ever do will be the work you do within the walls of your own home."[1] We believe that's true.

Of course, no one in this book did that perfectly, and that's another lesson to remember from each person's life: we are all learning. A true hero learns from his or her mistakes, changes for the better, and allows others to do the same.

We hope you will be inspired by the heroic deeds of the men and women in this book. Learn from them. Unlock your heroic potential. Be patient with yourself and others as you work to become. Care for your family, friends, and neighbors. Then, change the world!

You can make it a better place—and we know you will.

Sincerely,
Bushel & Peck Books

[1] Lee, Harold B. *The Teachings of Harold B. Lee.* 280.

HEROES BY SPECIAL POWER

While we hope you will read all the stories and meet all fifty of the real heroes in this book, we also know that every reader will have different interests. We're all unique, and the world needs all types of heroes. The list here shows each "Special Power" with its corresponding list of heroes. If you like art or music, for example, you might particularly enjoy the heroes under *Creativity*. Into sports? The heroes under *Fitness* might interest you.

COMPASSION
- Abraham Lincoln, 33
- Jon Huntsman Sr., 51
- Jonas Salk, 55
- Marie Curie, 61
- Yasuteru Yamada, 67
- Fred Rogers, 69
- "Stagecoach Mary" Fields, 73
- Georg Ferdinand Duckwitz, 75
- J. K. Rowling, 75
- Mother Teresa, 93
- Niels Bohr, 95
- Gail Halverson, 105

CONFIDENCE
- Sir Edmund Hillary, 37
- Kathrine Switzer, 41
- "Stagecoach Mary" Fields, 73
- Sarah Emma Edmonds, 97
- Sir Earnest Shackleton, 103

COURAGE
- Jackie Robinson, 19
- Todd Beamer, 27
- Malala Yousafzai, 31
- Corrie ten Boom, 49
- Caesar Rodney, 53
- César Chávez, 57
- Georg Ferdinand Duckwitz, 75
- Joshua Chamberlain, 81
- Sarah Emma Edmonds, 97
- Harriet Tubman, 101
- Sir Earnest Shackleton, 103
- William Tyndale, 107

CREATIVITY
- Dav Pilkey, 15
- Jim Henson, 25
- Jamie Oliver, 35
- J. J. Abrams, 43
- Fred Rogers, 69
- J. K. Rowling, 79
- Julia Child, 83
- Lin-Manuel Miranda, 87
- Ludwig van Beethoven, 89

CURIOSITY
- Mary Anning, 17
- Stephen Hawking, 21
- Jane Goodall, 39

EDUCATION
- Helen Keller, 23
- Malala Yousafzai, 31
- Booker T. Washington, 45
- Jonas Salk, 55
- Ellen Ochoa, 65
- William Tyndale, 107

FAMILY
- Malala Yousafzai, 31
- John Wooden, 47
- Chris Williams, 59
- Yasuteru Yamada, 67

FITNESS
- Jackie Robinson, 19
- Kathrine Switzer, 41
- John Wooden, 47
- Duke Kahanamoku, 63
- Iván Fernández, 77
- Shavarsh Vladimiri Karapetyan, 99

FORGIVENESS
- Corrie ten Boom, 49
- Chris Williams, 59

FRIENDSHIP	• Ralph Lazo, 13 • Jackie Robinson, 19 • Chris Williams, 59 • Gail Halverson, 105		
HARD WORK	• Helen Keller, 23 • Kathrine Switzer, 41 • Jon Huntsman Sr., 51 • Ellen Ochoa, 65	• "Stagecoach Mary" Fields, 73 • Lin-Manuel Miranda, 87	
HUMOR	• Dav Pilkey, 15 • Jim Henson, 25 • Julia Child, 83		
INDEPENDENCE	• Louis Braille, 29 • Caesar Rodney, 53 • Frederick Douglass, 71 • Mohandas Gandhi, 91		
INTEGRITY	• Jon Huntsman Sr., 51 • Georg Ferdinand Duckwitz, 75 • Iván Fernández, 77		
INTELLIGENCE	• Mary Anning, 17 • Stephen Hawking, 21 • Marie Curie, 61 • Katherine Johnson, 85	• Niels Bohr, 95	
JUSTICE	• William Wilberforce, 11 • Ralph Lazo, 13 • César Chávez, 57 • Frederick Douglass, 71		
LEADERSHIP	• William Wilberforce, 11 • Abraham Lincoln, 33 • Jamie Oliver, 35 • Booker T. Washington, 45	• John Wooden, 47 • César Chávez, 57 • Joshua Chamberlain, 81 • Mohandas Gandhi, 91	• Harriet Tubman, 101 • Sir Earnest Shackleton, 103
PATIENCE	• William Wilberforce, 11 • Mary Anning, 17 • Jane Goodall, 39		
PERSEVERANCE	• Dav Pilkey, 15 • Stephen Hawking, 21 • Helen Keller, 23 • Louis Braille, 29	• Sir Edmund Hillary, 37 • Katherine Johnson, 85 • Ludwig van Beethoven, 89	
SACRIFICE	• Todd Beamer, 27 • Abraham Lincoln, 33 • Yasuteru Yamada, 67 • Mohandas Gandhi, 91	• Mother Teresa, 93 • Shavarsh Vladimiri Karapetyan, 99 • William Tyndale, 107	

"I WILL GIVE
MY VOTE FOR
THE UTTER
ABOLITION OF
A TRADE WHICH
IS SHOCKING TO
HUMANITY . . .
AND REFLECTS
THE GREATEST
DISHONOR ON
THE BRITISH
. . . NATION."
—WILLIAM
WILBERFORCE

WILLIAM WILBERFORCE

1759–1833

SPECIAL POWERS:	LEADERSHIP	JUSTICE	PATIENCE

William grew up in Hull, England, near the North Sea where his grandfather was a wealthy shipping merchant. William had a wonderful singing voice and loved to speak at social gatherings.

He loved school and was happy at home until his father died when William was nine. His mother sent him to live with a wealthy uncle and aunt in London. William grew close to his new family who were very religious. He was sad when his mother made him come home two years later. William wrote letters to his uncle and aunt, telling them how much he missed them, their kindness, and their love of God.

Back home, William's mother took him to parties and let him have fun with friends. It took him several years to adapt to this new party-life. His mother wanted him to develop important social connections, but he longed for the way his uncle and aunt had loved him simply for the goodness in his soul.

After he graduated from Cambridge, William became a member of the British Parliament. He decided that he could socialize like his mother wanted, but that he needed to help people also. He and his friends heard a lot of stories about how many slaves died on the British ships from Africa to the West Indies. He learned that the owners were cruel to their slaves. Since William was such a good speaker, his friends in Parliament wanted him to work to abolish slavery in the British colonies. William agreed and began the fight.

William helped support a community in Sierra Leone, West Africa, where people of every color lived together. African tribal chiefs and the community leaders worked to keep ships from taking more slaves.

William also gave speeches in Parliament about abolishing slavery in England and justice for Africans. It took many long years, but by 1807, he had won his first victory when England made it illegal to sell or ship slaves. That didn't end slavery entirely, so William kept fighting. But every time he proposed an antislavery bill, powerful slave owners voted against it. They wanted men to harvest sugarcane and tobacco.

William and his friends never gave up. They knew they would have to be patient and keep trying. Finally, three days before William died in 1833, enough people had come to agree with William that the British government made final negotiations to pass an antislavery bill. William's leadership had at long last brought about justice. He was buried in Westminster Abby so that everyone could remember his kindness to all people.

William was born with wealth, position, and talent—things that many people spend their whole lives chasing because they think it will make them happy. But William knew that life was about something greater. He felt a higher calling to make a difference in the lives of others. William used all he had been given to make that happen—and it did.

YOU CAN BE A HERO	Have you ever met people in your life who were bullied? What could you do to help them? And, what do you think you could do to help the bullies?

"INTERNMENT
WAS IMMORAL.
IT WAS WRONG,
AND I COULDN'T
ACCEPT IT."
–RALPH LAZO

RALPH LAZO

1924–1992

SPECIAL POWERS:	FRIENDSHIP	JUSTICE

R alph grew up in a Los Angeles neighborhood with Japanese, Filipino, Jewish, Korean, Mexican, and Chinese kids. He was Irish and Latino himself. His mother died when he was little, and his father was away much of the time working. So, Ralph grew up in the homes of his friends. They were his family.

Ralph was in high school when World War II broke out. On December 7, 1941, the Japanese attacked Pearl Harbor. President Franklin D. Roosevelt signed an executive order that sent Japanese people in the United States to internment camps. Over 110,000 Japanese—most of them United States citizens—were ordered to camps in the desolate deserts of the United States.

Ralph was very upset that his friends had to go away. So, he told his father he was going to summer camp. Instead, he got on a bus to the Manzanar internment camp in Owens Valley, California, where his Japanese friends were. The people there slept on straw mattresses and had no privacy. In the summer, the heat soared to 110 degrees, and in the winter, the cold dropped to near freezing.

When Ralph got to camp, he made friends with everyone. He was elected high school class president and was a cheerleader. He worked hard while he was there, planting trees, delivering mail, and helping with parties to keep everyone's spirits high.

He had to leave the camp in 1944 because he was drafted into the army and sent to the South Pacific. There, he received a Bronze Star for bravery.

After the war, the camps were closed, but Ralph never forgot his friends—they were still like his family. He wrote them letters and called them up to make sure they were going to vote. He became a teacher, working with children with special needs and helping Latino youth go to college.

Ralph raised money for a lawsuit against the government because they had sent the Japanese to internment camps during World War II. He was happy when, years later, President Reagan signed a law that awarded each person who survived the camps $20,000. Congress also apologized to the Japanese and said that the camps were based on "race prejudice, war hysteria, and failure of political leadership."

When the whole world turned against Ralph's friends, he stood up for them and fought for justice. He showed that friendship could withstand the toughest times—even a world war.

YOU CAN BE A HERO	Ralph's commitment to his friends strengthened their relationship. What could you do to strengthen the friendships you have?

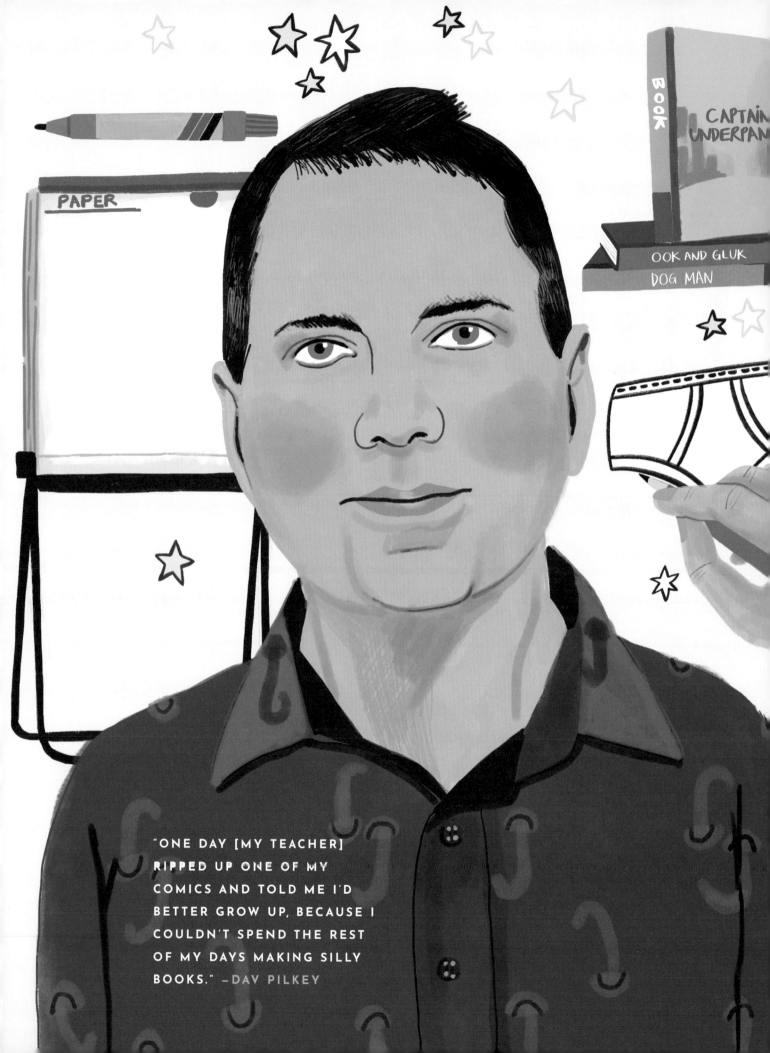

PAPER

BOOK

CAPTAIN
UNDERPAN

OOK AND GLUK
DOG MAN

"ONE DAY [MY TEACHER]
RIPPED UP ONE OF MY
COMICS AND TOLD ME I'D
BETTER GROW UP, BECAUSE I
COULDN'T SPEND THE REST
OF MY DAYS MAKING SILLY
BOOKS." –DAV PILKEY

DAV PILKEY

1966 –

SPECIAL POWERS:	CREATIVITY	PERSEVERANCE	HUMOR

Dav created lots of popular children's books, including the Captain Underpants and Dog Man series. His name is spelled a funny way because when he worked at Pizza Hut as a teenager, the e was left off his nametag. It's been Dav ever since!

As a boy, he had a hard time sitting and concentrating in school. He got into trouble for cracking jokes and flying paper airplanes. He was diagnosed with attention-deficit/hyperactivity disorder (ADHD) and dyslexia and spent a lot of time sitting at a desk in the hallway outside his classroom. Dav spent hours doodling and making up funny stories, including ones about underpants. He got the idea when his teacher talked about underpants in class and everyone laughed. She told them not to laugh, and the kids laughed harder! His classmates *loved* his comics—but his teacher and principal didn't. They told him he wouldn't amount to anything if he kept making up silly stories.

Fortunately, Dav didn't listen. He persisted in drawing and writing anyway. Dav's parents liked his drawings and his writing. When he told his mom about his school troubles, she would say, "Maybe some good will come of this." So Dav tried harder. He didn't give up on his books. When he was eighteen years old, he wrote and illustrated a children's book called *World War Won*. It won a national publication contest and his career as an author-illustrator had officially begun. His teachers at Kent State University believed in him and told him to keep writing, so he studied everything he could about children's books.

Dav never forgot about the underpants that made everyone laugh. When he was older, he created the Captain Underpants series for kids and, sure enough, it made everyone laugh—just like it did when he was a boy. He's written lots of other books, including *Dog Man*, *Super Diaper Baby*, *Ook and Gluck*, *The Paper Boy*, *Dog Breath*, *Dumb Bunnies*, *Mighty Robot*, and many others.

Sometimes, people say you can't do things. Dave was persistent and did them anyway. Not only did he keep doing what he loved, but his creativity and humor helped children all over the world find a way to love reading.

YOU CAN BE A HERO	Dav struggled in school because he had ADHD and dyslexia. Is it possible those weaknesses were actually strengths that helped him become a children's author? Think about weaknesses you might have and how you could turn them into strengths, too.

"THE CARPENTER'S DAUGHTER HAS WON A NAME FOR HERSELF, AND DESERVED TO WIN IT." —CHARLES DICKENS

MARY ANNING

1799–1847

SPECIAL POWERS:	CURIOSITY	INTELLIGENCE	PATIENCE

Mary Anning and her brother, Joseph, loved to walk with their father along the cliffs by the seashore near their home in Lyme Regis, England. The Atlantic winds blew cold and blustery, but Mary didn't notice as they studied the cliffs, looking for "snake stones"—fossils. Her father was a carpenter but hunted for fossils as a side business. Sometimes the rocks on the cliffs fell away and fossils were exposed. People bought these because they thought they had magical powers. Mary and her brother also found "verteberries"—vertebrae—that looked like giant backbones.

Mary was a sickly child, so her nurse took her for walks because she thought the fresh air would do her good. One day, a sudden thunderstorm came up. The nurse huddled with Mary under a tree. Lightning hit the tree and Mary was knocked unconscious. Mary was rushed back to the house, and her parents put her in a bath of warm water. Soon she opened her eyes. Her parents and the doctor called it a miracle. Mary was strong and healthy from then on.

After her father died, Mary took over the business of hunting for fossils. Great discoveries were rare, and it took a great deal of patience to keep searching. When she was twelve, her brother found a large fossil that looked like a lizard's head. It was four feet long and had large eyeholes and two hundred teeth. He told Mary to sell it because the family needed money. Mary patiently hunted until she found the rest of the skeleton. It had a snout like a swordfish, teeth like a crocodile, flippers like a dolphin, and the spine of a fish. The creature that looked like a fish-lizard was named an *Ichthyosaurus* and placed in the British Museum. But since Mary was a woman, no one gave her credit for it at the time.

Mary sometimes guided visitors on fossil hunts. William Buckland, from Oxford, and Henry De la Beche, a friend, loved scouring the cliffs with her. She read geology books and dissected small animals. Once, Mary even found a *Plesiosaurus*. George Cuvier, considered the father of paleontology, thought the fossil was a fake at first. But after he saw it, he said it was "amazing."

After her death, Mary began to be recognized for her contributions to science. Henry De la Beche, president of the Geological Society of London, honored Mary after her death with a speech—the only one ever given for someone who was not a member of the society.

Today, Mary has fossils in the British Museum of Natural History in London, the Museum of Natural History in Paris, and the Academy of Natural Sciences of Philadelphia, among other places. Her patient work, fueled by her curiosity and intelligence, had unearthed the secrets of the past. And in showing the world what women could do, perhaps she revealed the greatest secret of all.

YOU CAN BE A HERO	Many people didn't give Mary credit for her discoveries because she was a woman. How could you help someone get recognized for the good they did?

"LIFE IS NOT A SPECTATOR SPORT. . . . IF YOU'RE GOING TO SPEND YOUR WHOLE LIFE IN THE GRANDSTAND JUST WATCHING WHAT GOES ON, IN MY OPINION, YOU'RE WASTING YOUR LIFE."
–JACKIE ROBINSON

JACKIE ROBINSON

1919–1972

SPECIAL POWERS:	COURAGE	FITNESS	FRIENDSHIP

Jackie Robinson grew up in a poor family in Georgia. He was the youngest of five kids who all loved to play sports. His family moved to California where he attended college at UCLA. There, he joined the baseball, basketball, football, and track teams. He was the first UCLA athlete to letter in four sports. After college, he played football in Hawaii and Los Angeles and was then drafted into the military during World War II. After the war, he played baseball for the Negro leagues, which were baseball teams formed by African Americans because the other national teams wouldn't allow black players.

That all changed when Branch Rickey, president of the Brooklyn Dodgers, asked Jackie to play for his team. At that time, there were still no black players in major league baseball. Jackie would have to endure the taunting and mocking that white spectators might pitch at him. Was he brave enough to help break down the walls of segregation? Jackie told Branch Rickey, "Yes." On April 15, 1947, Jackie took his place on Ebbets Field as first baseman for the Brooklyn Dodgers. He scored the winning run that day.

When crowds of baseball fans jeered at him because his skin was a different color than theirs, Jackie stood tall and let the hurtful words hurl by him like foul balls. At a Cincinnati game, Jackie and Pee Wee Reese, a white teammate, stood side-by-side and resolutely faced down the heckling fans. They sent their courage out into the stadium. The fans quieted down. Many people at the game remember that day because they saw an example of true friendship. Years later, the story would become a symbol of brotherhood to a nation still struggling to overlook differences and come together.

At the end of his first season, Jackie was voted National League Rookie of the Year. He and his team won the World Series in 1955 where he even stole home base—something no one ever did. He was inducted into the Baseball Hall of Fame in 1962.

Because of his courage, Jackie opened the door for African Americans to play in all major league sports. He had endured mocking, taunting, and bullying, and done so with patience and strength. Best of all, he and Pee Wee had showed that people of any color could be friends.

YOU CAN BE A HERO	Sometimes, people exclude others because they don't like something about them. It could be the color of their skin, their gender, their religion, or even how much money they make. What could you do to be inclusive instead?

"MY GOAL IS SIMPLE:
IT IS A COMPLETE
UNDERSTANDING OF
THE UNIVERSE, WHY
IT IS AS IT IS, AND
WHY IT EXISTS AT
ALL."
—STEPHEN HAWKING

STEPHEN HAWKING

1942–2018

SPECIAL POWERS:	INTELLIGENCE	PERSEVERANCE	CURIOSITY

Stephen Hawking's teachers thought he was a slacker because he didn't do his schoolwork. But his friends knew otherwise, often calling him "Einstein." Stephen was born on the 300th anniversary of Galileo's death—a remarkable connection for two scientists who studied the universe.

As a boy, Stephen loved reading. He and his family read during dinner every night. He and his friends made up board games—one of them had 4,000 squares. They made fireworks and even built a computer out of old clock and machine parts.

At age seventeen, he took the entrance exams for Oxford University in England, scoring so high on the physics part of the exam that he won a scholarship. But when he went to school there, he was bored with his classes because he already knew the information. So, he joined the Oxford rowing team. He was the coxswain (the person who steers the boat and shouts commands to keep the rowers moving together). He spent more time with the rowing team than he did on his studies, but he still passed his exams to graduate and went on to Cambridge University to do research in cosmology (the study of the formation and development of the universe).

During his first year at Cambridge, his speech became slurred and his family noticed that he stumbled a lot. Doctors diagnosed him with ALS, or Lou Gehrig's disease, as the cause of his deteriorating muscles. Before his illness, he had thought life was boring. Now he decided to persevere to get as much out of life as he could.

Stephen was curious about everything in the universe. He became engrossed in his research and studied black holes, which can be formed by dying stars. He found they could explode. This was new information, and one scientist called it "absolute rubbish." But Stephen proved his theory, and soon, scientists named the particles left from the explosions "Hawking radiation."

Stephen was given a professorship at Cambridge that Sir Isaac Newton had held in 1669. Because of his ALS, Stephen's muscles had deteriorated so much that he couldn't talk, but still he persevered. Scientists created a computer that helped him talk so he could continue to teach and give speeches. Everyone loved to hear him lecture because he had asked a lot of interesting questions about the universe, and he had found answers to many of these questions.

Stephen died in 2018. His remarkable intelligence and curiosity had changed the way the world thought about the universe. And his perseverance? That changed how the world thought about life. No matter what happens with illness, tragedy, or disappointment, one's life is always a precious gift to share.

YOU CAN BE A HERO	Stephen loved asking questions and discovering new ideas. What are you interested in? Can you ask questions and discover new things?

"I HAVE THE ADVANTAGE OF A MIND TRAINED TO THINK, AND THAT IS THE DIFFERENCE BETWEEN MYSELF AND MOST PEOPLE, NOT MY BLINDNESS AND THEIR SIGHT."
—HELEN KELLER

HELEN KELLER

1880–1968

| SPECIAL POWERS: | PERSEVERANCE | EDUCATION | HARD WORK |

Helen Keller began life on a farm with pigs and chickens. As a baby, she loved hearing the birds sing and seeing the red petals of the rose. But before she was two years old, she became ill with a high fever. Her parents worried that she might die. Fortunately, she did recover, but from then on she couldn't see or hear. Her world was now darkness and silence.

Her parents searched for doctors who were trained to help, but no one knew what to do. Then, when Helen was seven, Anne Sullivan from the Perkins Institution for the Blind in Boston, Massachusetts, came to Helen's home in Tuscumbia, Alabama. By this time, Helen had become a wild child, eating food off everyone's plates and throwing temper tantrums.

Anne used sign language to spell words like *doll* and *cake* on Helen's hand, but Helen didn't understand. She still had temper tantrums. Then one day, Anne spelled w-a-t-e-r on Helen's palm while she ran water over her other hand. Helen finally understood. The finger game spelled words! Helen was so excited that she learned thirty words that day.

Anne taught Helen more sign language and how to read braille with her fingers. She also learned to write letters with a pencil and paper on a board with grooves. When Helen was eight, she and Anne traveled to Boston to the Perkins Institution. Helen played with other children and found lots of braille books to read. She learned very quickly. People wrote articles about her, and she became famous.

Helen wanted to learn to talk. No one thought she could do it. First, she had to learn to read lips. Helen put her middle finger on her teacher's nose, her forefinger on her teacher's lips, and her thumb on her teacher's throat. As the teacher spoke, Anne spelled each word into Helen's other hand. Helen learned to read lips. Now she could learn to talk. She practiced and practiced making the sounds. Her speech was never very clear, but she worked at it until people could understand her.

She wanted to go to college. No one thought she could do that, either. There were many obstacles. She couldn't see or hear the teacher, so Anne had to spell everything into Helen's hand. Sometimes Anne couldn't keep up with the teacher's words. Also, college textbooks weren't written in braille. Anne had to finger-spell or read them out loud to Helen. It was hard, but Helen graduated from college with honors.

She became famous because she worked hard to do things that no one thought she could do. She wrote books, gave speeches all over the world, and met world leaders, including several presidents of the United States. Helen taught the world that anything could be accomplished—if only you had the perseverance.

| YOU CAN BE A HERO | Helen persisted with her goals and studied hard. What kind of goals do you have? How can you work toward them? |

"WHEN I WAS YOUNG, MY AMBITION WAS TO BE ONE OF THE PEOPLE WHO MADE A DIFFERENCE IN THIS WORLD."
—JIM HENSON

JIM HENSON

1936–1990

SPECIAL POWERS:	CREATIVITY	HUMOR

Jim Henson loved to make his grandmother laugh. He would tell her funny stories and draw her pictures while they sat on the front porch of their home in Leland, Mississippi. On lazy summer days, Jim floated on the Mississippi River with his best friend, Kermit, and played ping-pong. His first and forever favorite movie was *The Wizard of Oz* because the Lion, the Tin Man, and the Scarecrow were like life-sized puppets.

Jim's family moved to Maryland where he published a cartoon in a newspaper when he was only thirteen. His father wanted him to study science in college, but Jim didn't think that was as fun as making puppets in the art classes he took. He cut up his mom's old green coat to make his first Kermit the Frog puppet and gave him eyes out of ping-pong balls cut in half. Jim made Kermit's eyes look slightly crossed because he thought they were funny that way.

Later, Jim and his wife, Jane, created friends for Kermit: the Muppets. They did lots of television commercials and even appeared on *The Ed Sullivan Show*. A television producer named Joan Cooney asked him to be on a children's show with a funny name: *Sesame Street*. He told her he'd do it. He wanted the show to be funny, not preachy. He wanted to make kids laugh.

Jim, with help from other puppeteer friends, brought Kermit the Frog, Oscar the Grouch, Bert and Ernie, Big Bird, and Grover to life. Jim had to crouch down below the camera, hold his arms in the air until they cramped, and use his voice in lots of funny ways. But he didn't care. He loved doing it because his puppets could be best friends with children and adults all over the world.

He went on to be part of other television shows like *Saturday Night Live*. He helped create Yoda, the Jedi Master in *Star Wars: The Empire Strikes Back*. Jim also made *The Muppet Show*, starring Kermit and Miss Piggy and famous celebrities of the day, but that wasn't enough for Miss Piggy—she wanted to be a movie star. And so, Jim produced *The Muppet Movie* and many more films like it.

From the porches of Sesame Street to the lights of Muppet Studios, Jim's creations have brought joy to countless individuals. He used his creativity and humor to make the whole world smile—even Miss Piggy.

YOU CAN BE A HERO	Jim loved to create stories and puppets that made people laugh. He brought joy to many people. How can you bring joy to those around you?

"LET'S ROLL."
-TODD BEAMER

TODD BEAMER

1968–2001

SPECIAL POWERS:	COURAGE	SACRIFICE

No matter what happened, Todd Beamer had the courage to stay cool in a crisis.

He grew up outside Chicago. As a child, his parents taught him to pray. Todd figured out that if he said very long prayers, his bedtime would be later. So, with his mother sitting by his side, he blessed everything in the house—the windows, the mirrors, the floors, and more. His mother laughed about it later.

From the time Todd was little, he enjoyed sports—especially baseball. But no matter what sport he played, he had the courage to stay cool when the pressure was on to win. He could dribble the basketball between his opponent's legs or hit a grand slam home run in a baseball game.

Years later, Todd's faith and cool head would change the course of history. On September 11, 2001, Todd was on United Flight 93, which was hijacked along with two other planes that hit the World Trade Center in New York City and a third that crashed into the Pentagon in Washington, DC. The hijackers of Flight 93 took over the plane and wanted to slam it into the United States Capitol building or into the White House where the president lived.

Todd and some of the other passengers huddled in the back of the plane. He called the airphone supervisor and told her that they were going to take the plane back from the hijackers. Then, he took a deep breath and asked the other passengers to join him in reciting the 23rd Psalm and the Lord's Prayer. Todd remained calm—even though he and the others knew they would die because there was no one to land the plane. They would have to give their lives to save others.

Todd's last brave words to the group before they stormed the cockpit were, "Let's roll!" They overpowered the hijackers, took the plane back, and crashed it into the ground in Shanksville, Pennsylvania, before the hijackers could reach their targets in Washington, DC.

Todd's courageous sacrifice saved the country from a terrible tragedy. He and many others gave their lives so that many more could continue to live in freedom.

YOU CAN BE A HERO	Todd helped his country remain free. What can you do to show you value freedom?

BRAILLE

"IF MY EYES WILL NOT TELL
ME ABOUT MEN AND EVENTS,
IDEAS AND DOCTRINES, I MUST
FIND ANOTHER WAY."
–LOUIS BRAILLE

LOUIS BRAILLE

1809–1852

SPECIAL POWERS:	PERSEVERANCE	INDEPENDENCE

From the time Louis was a little boy, he wanted to be independent and do things for himself. His father owned a leather shop in Coupvray, a small town in northern France, where he made saddles, harnesses, and other goods. Louis loved to play with scraps of leather in his father's shop, but he longed to try out the tools. One day, when no one else was around, young Louis climbed up on the workbench and grabbed a pointed awl. He started to poke a hole in the leather but missed and hit his eye. It bled and became infected. The infection spread to his other eye, and soon, Louis was blind.

Over time, Louis figured out ways to do things just like sighted people. He learned to count the steps from the house to the barn, and he followed the smell of baking bread to the bakery. As he grew older, he went to school and listened carefully so he could recite the teacher's lessons. His brother hammered nails into a board to represent the letters of the alphabet, and his sister taught him to make words.

When Louis was ten years old, he went to Paris to a school for the blind. Even though he was young himself, he helped the students become as independent as they could. One day, a soldier came in with bumps on a paper—dots and dashes used to send messages that could be read with one's fingers at night when there was no light. Louis thought this would be a great way for the blind to be able to read books by themselves. He decided to make a system of dots and dashes for the students. But the teachers didn't like this idea. It wasn't the way they were used to teaching, and besides, Louis was "too young" to change things.

So, Louis continued his studies and practiced his music. He loved to play the organ and became an organist at Saint-Nicholas-des-Champs, one of the largest cathedrals in Paris.

But he never forgot about his idea to help the blind read with the bumpy dots and dashes. A few years later, he graduated and became a teacher at the school. He showed the students how to read with his new system, and they were thrilled. They told others about the dots and dashes, and soon, many blind people were reading books on their own. Louis's perseverance and determination to be independent opened the magic of books to blind people of the whole world. And today, his new reading system has been given the perfect name: *braille*.

YOU CAN BE A HERO	Louis didn't let his blindness keep him from being independent. How are you learning to do things on your own so you can become independent?

MALALA YOUSAFZAI

1997–

SPECIAL POWERS:	EDUCATION	COURAGE	FAMILY

Malala was born into a family that believed in education for all children, including girls. Her father, Ziauddin, wanted Malala to read and write so she could learn all about the world. She and her little brother, Khushal, played in her father's school just across the street from their home. They loved the green of the valleys and snowcapped mountains of their home in Pakistan.

A group of military people in their country called the Taliban didn't like education—especially for girls. They were a terrorist group that scared people by telling them they were wicked for listening to music and for using computers.

When Malala was only eleven years old, she gave a speech against the Taliban, telling everyone that girls needed to be educated as well as boys. Malala and her friends were angry when the Taliban wouldn't let them go to school. The terrorists hurt people and burned down schools, but that didn't stop Malala.

The British Broadcasting Corporation (BBC) wanted Malala to write a blog. Her father sent them Malala's diary about a girl's life in Pakistan. They posted it online under a different name, Gul Makai, because it was dangerous for Malala to speak out. Soon people all over the world came to love Gul Makai. But the Taliban continued to hurt people.

Malala was chosen to be the speaker of a children's group connected with the Khpal Kor Foundation, a group that helps boys and girls in Pakistan. She talked about the rights of children. The government of Pakistan could see all the good she was doing and gave her the National Youth Peace Prize. With the prize money, she established a foundation to help girls get an education. The *New York Times* did a video article about Malala. More and more people heard her story. But the Taliban weren't happy.

On October 9, 2012, a gunman stopped Malala's school bus and shot his gun at her. One bullet entered the left side of Malala's brain and lodged in her shoulder. Two other girls were hurt, too. The bus driver sped to the nearest hospital, but the doctors there didn't have the equipment to help Malala. So, they flew her to England. Cards and letters poured in from all over the world. Malala recovered, and continued to speak out for the rights of children.

In 2013, Malala was awarded a Nobel Peace Prize. She was the youngest person ever to receive the honor. Her foundation continued to grow and help children in Syria, Lebanon, Nigeria, and other places.

On July 12, 2013, her sixteenth birthday, the United Nations established Malala Day as a time to remember that all children should be able to go to school, to learn to read and write, and to be free.

With the support of her family and with great courage, Malala faced down the Taliban to fight for education. She believed that books, not bullets, would change the word—and she was right.

YOU CAN BE A HERO	Malala loved to learn. Education was important to her. How did she help other children value learning? Can you do the same?

"WHATEVER YOU ARE, BE A GOOD ONE."
—ABRAHAM LINCOLN

ABRAHAM LINCOLN

1809–1865

SPECIAL POWERS:	LEADERSHIP	COMPASSION	SACRIFICE

Abraham Lincoln loved to learn about new things. Ideas were important to him. He grew up in Kentucky where there was so much work to do on the farm that he and his sister, Sarah, didn't go to school very often. But that didn't stop Lincoln. He read as much as he could and was often found under a tree with his feet propped up on the trunk and a book in his hands.

When Lincoln was seven, the family moved to Indiana. His father liked living there because the law didn't allow slaves. Lincoln also felt that slavery should be illegal. He couldn't stand to see anything hurt. Once, when the family moved to Decatur, Illinois, Abe's little dog fell through the ice on the river. Lincoln plunged into the water and saved it.

When he was older, Lincoln became interested in serving in the government. Lincoln ran for the Illinois state legislature and lost. He tried a second time and won a seat in the Illinois House of Representatives. To do his job, he needed to learn about the law, so he borrowed some law books and headed for the state capital. He served four terms, and by then, he had studied enough law books to become a lawyer. He moved to Springfield, Illinois, opened a law office, and became a circuit court judge.

He won a seat in the US House of Representatives and went to Washington. He couldn't understand how Washington, DC, permitted slavery in a country where all men were created equal. So Lincoln ran for the US Senate against Stephen A. Douglas, one of the country's most famous politicians. Though Lincoln lost, he began making a name for himself and spoke powerfully about the need to keep the United States strong.

A young girl, Grace Bedell from New York, wrote a letter to Lincoln, suggesting he would look better if he grew a beard. So, he did. Lincoln then ran for President of the United States and won in 1860. When he made a speech in New York, he asked if Grace was in the audience. She was, and he gave her a kiss.

Just after he moved into the White House, the Civil War broke out. Lincoln studied all he could about military strategies and tried to help his armies. He welcomed visitors and talked to each person that came in. He listened to his advisors and asked the very best people to help him, even if they hadn't been kind to him in the past.

Near the end of the war, Lincoln helped pass the Thirteenth Amendment. It was a new law that outlawed slavery in the United States. It freed anyone who was a slave. Church bells everywhere rang to celebrate new freedom for all people.

But, just after he won reelection, Lincoln was shot by John Wilkes Booth at Ford's Theater. Lincoln died shortly after, and the country mourned his loss. A funeral train carried Lincoln back to Illinois to be buried. Eleven funerals were held in his honor across the country. Abe's leadership and compassion had saved the country and freed the slaves. He sacrificed his life, along with 620,000 others, for the future of the United States.

YOU CAN BE A HERO	Lincoln wanted everyone to be treated equal. What can you do to make sure those around you are treated fairly?

"I COULD COOK FROM QUITE AN EARLY AGE—PURELY BECAUSE I LIKED IT." –JAMIE OLIVER

JAMIE OLIVER

1975–

SPECIAL POWERS:	CREATIVITY	LEADERSHIP	HARD WORK

Jamie grew up thinking his life was just like that of Tom Sawyer or Huckleberry Finn in Mark Twain's novels. He and his friends lived near a river and loved to fish and get into scrapes. One time, he and his buddy left their boat by the river and went home for dinner. When they came back, they found a lady screaming near the boat. Jamie had left the lid off his jar of maggots that he used for fishing bait, and worms were crawling all over the boat!

Growing up in Clavering, Essex, with rolling green hills and a meandering river seemed like an ideal carefree life. But there in rural England, Jamie learned to work hard. His father and mother owned the town pub, called the Cricketers, where the village people came to eat—and Jamie went to work. First he learned to wash dishes, and then he graduated to peeling potatoes and carrots. Soon he was standing on a chair to help his mom cook. One morning, when he decided to sleep in, his father turned the garden hose on, shoved it through Jamie's bedroom window, and squirted him awake. It was Saturday and there was work to do.

Jamie struggled in school because he had dyslexia. When he had finally had enough of school, he enrolled in Westminster Kingsway College in London to learn to be a chef. From there, he went to France for further study and then on to work with Gennaro Contaldo to learn to make Italian pasta and bread.

He got a job at the River Café, an upscale restaurant in London. When the BBC filmed a Christmas cooking special there, Jamie was in the background preparing vegetables for the chefs. When the producers saw the tape, they liked Jamie's hustle so much that they offered him his own cooking show. They called it *The Naked Chef*. Jamie hated the name because he didn't want people to think he was naked. It was really the food and cooking techniques that were stripped down to the plain essentials—naked. Despite the name, people loved Jamie's show and creative cooking.

From there, Jamie went on to write cookbooks and do other shows. He also prepared food for the British Prime Minister, Tony Blair, and his foreign visitors at 10 Downing Street. His show gained fame in America and he became wealthy. But Jamie wanted to do more than be a famous chef—he wanted to make a difference. He used his money to train troubled youths to become chefs to give them a better future. He also helped to reform school lunches for British children and campaigned for healthy eating and whole foods. With his culinary creativity and leadership skills, Jamie will continue to fight for causes he loves so that people might have a better quality of life.

YOU CAN BE A HERO	Jamie learned to work hard when he was little. How can you work hard each day?

"IT'S NOT THE
MOUNTAIN WE
CONQUER, BUT
OURSELVES."
–SIR EDMUND
HILLARY

SIR EDMUND HILLARY

1919–1972

SPECIAL POWERS: CONFIDENCE   PERSEVERANCE

Edmund grew up in New Zealand. When he was young, he didn't like school very much. He would rather be outside in the wind and sunshine.

Edmund grew up tall—six feet, two inches—and strong. But, like he had since he was a boy, Edmund doubted himself. His father had been very unkind, and Edmund grew up with little confidence.

In college, he became interested in hiking, so he joined the Auckland University Tramping Club. During that time, he found a positive-thinking group where he finally found his confidence—even enough confidence to scale tall mountains. He climbed the tallest mountains of New Zealand and dreamed of hiking Mt. Everest, the highest mountain in the world—over five miles up.

Everest, the giant of rock, snow, and ice, loomed above the other tall mountains of the Himalayas. Ten expeditions had failed to climb the mountain so far. Nineteen men had been buried under avalanche snow, or had fallen through a crevasse, or had slipped off a cliff to their deaths. But in 1953, Edmund decided to try it himself. He became climbing partners with Tenzing Norgay, a man from Nepal, so that they could keep each other from falling. The expedition took three months. The trail up to the mountain was 190 miles long, and it was almost a month before they reached the base of the mountain. Edmund and Tenzing had to have 400 men help them because they needed 22,000 pounds of equipment and supplies.

Soon, it was time to leave their basecamp and ascend the mountain. Edmund and Tenzing strapped spikes on their boots and used ice axes to chop steps into the ice so they wouldn't fall. When they found wide cracks in the glaciers, they placed ladders across them and crawled over. On the way up, Edmund slipped into a crevasse, and Tenzing pulled him out. Edmund chopped more ice steps as they inched up the mountain. They eventually had to put on their oxygen masks because the air was so thin. Tenzing's line to his oxygen tank froze, and he couldn't breathe. Edmund helped him free the ice so he could get air again. They came to a rock cliff and could see no way to climb it. Edmund squeezed between the cliff and an ice wall and pushed his way to the top. Tenzing followed.

Finally, they reached the summit. They waved the flags they had on their ice axes and took pictures. They couldn't stay long because they didn't want their oxygen supply to run out. The date was May 29, 1953. It was the day Queen Elizabeth of England was crowned—a coronation present.

When Edmund got back to England, Queen Elizabeth made him a knight. He trekked to the North and South Poles also and established a foundation to build schools and hospitals in the Himalayan region. With perseverance and his newfound confidence, Edmund had accomplished great feats for the world and found that he could stand tall—as tall as Everest.

YOU CAN BE A HERO	Edmund didn't have much confidence in himself when he was young. Over time, he found ways to feel good about himself. What can you do to feel good about yourself?

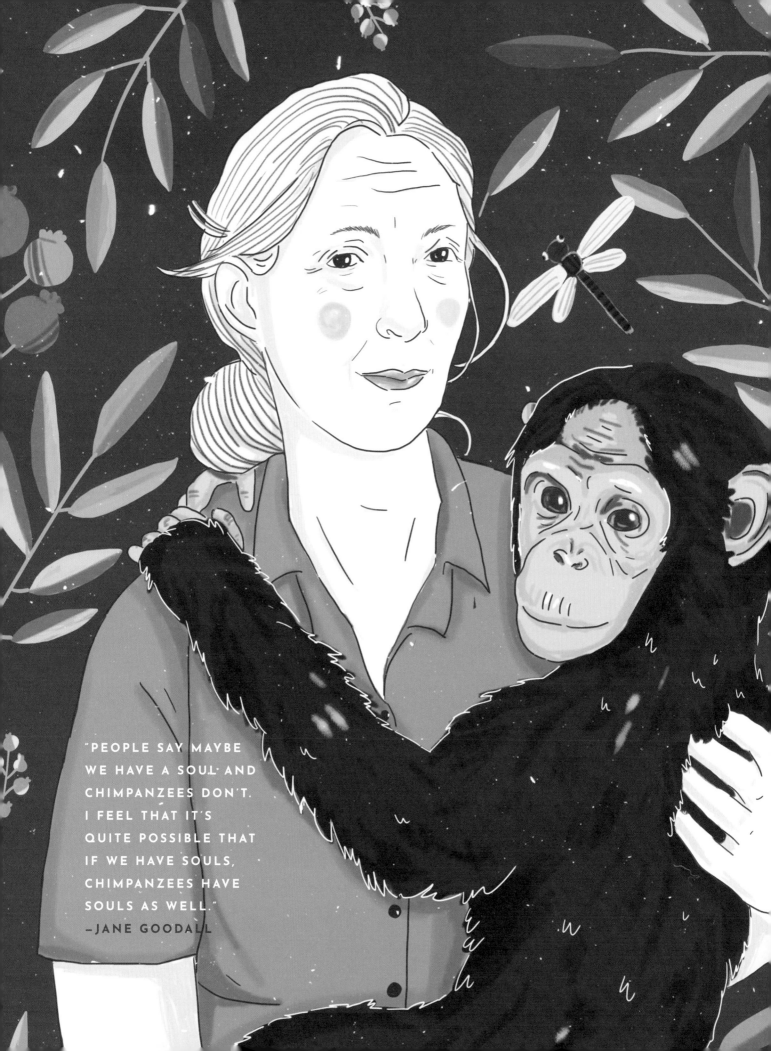

"PEOPLE SAY MAYBE
WE HAVE A SOUL AND
CHIMPANZEES DON'T.
I FEEL THAT IT'S
QUITE POSSIBLE THAT
IF WE HAVE SOULS,
CHIMPANZEES HAVE
SOULS AS WELL."
—JANE GOODALL

JANE GOODALL

1934–

| SPECIAL POWERS: | CURIOSITY | PATIENCE |

Jane loved to learn about the world of animals. One day, her mother couldn't find her and was about ready to call the police when Jane, very excited, came running into the house. She told her mother that chicken eggs come out of hens between their legs! Jane had hidden herself in the hen house, quiet as could be, and watched patiently until a hen laid an egg. She wanted to find out about animals from all over the world, but for now, she had to content herself with studying squirrels and birds in her neighborhood.

Jane had a faithful companion—a dog named Rusty who lived up the road with his owner. The dog spent every day with Jane, and she taught him to sit with a biscuit on his nose and jump through hoops. She learned a lot about animal behavior from Rusty.

After finishing school, she applied to be a secretary because her family didn't have enough money to send her to college. But her dream was to visit Africa. She finally got her chance when a friend, Clo, wrote to her from Kenya and invited Jane to visit. Jane saved every penny to buy her passage on a ship to Kenya. There, she found a job working for Louis Leakey, an anthropologist. She told him she wanted to study chimpanzees in the wild. He agreed to find the money for her to begin her research in a place called Gombe in Tanzania.

She met with a zoologist, George Schaller, who told Jane that if she could see chimps eating meat or using a tool, her research would be a success. Jane spent hours observing the chimps in the wild. Her patience paid off. After three weeks, she saw a chimp break a twig from a bush, pull off the leaves, poke it into an anthill, and eat the ants off the stick. The chimps were eating meat—the ants—and using a tool—the stick!

She wrote scientific papers on her research. *National Geographic* sent a photographer to document her findings. Now there was money for her to go to college. She split her time between Africa and England for her studies. She earned a PhD in ethology, the study of animal behavior.

Jane not only studied chimps in the wild, but she also created a foundation to study chimps in zoos and to monitor research projects involving chimps. She campaigned to have the animals treated well. She was named Messenger of Peace by the United Nations. She has written many books, established the Jane Goodall Institute, and founded Roots and Shoots, a conservation program for children.

Because of Jane's curiosity and patience, the world knows more about chimpanzees than ever before. And when you know something, you can finally love it and protect it—just as Jane does.

| YOU CAN BE A HERO | Jane taught the world to love and protect the chimpanzees. What do you love? How could you protect it? |

KATHRINE SWITZER

1947–

SPECIAL POWERS:	CONFIDENCE	FITNESS	HARD WORK

Kathrine Switzer loved to run. As a child, she ran whenever she could. But in high school, she decided to be a cheerleader because girls weren't allowed to participate in sports—even running. People said girls were too fragile and weak.

When she was in college, her father suggested that she join the track team rather than just watch sports as a cheerleader. There were no track teams for girls, so she joined the men's team at Syracuse University.

Her coach, Arnie Briggs, loved to tell stories about his participation in the Boston Marathon. Kathrine trained with Arnie and listened to his stories. She decided she wanted to run the famous 26.2-mile race herself. Arnie told her that twenty-six miles was too far for a woman to run, but Kathrine said she could do it. She and Arnie set a practice course, and they began running the twenty-six miles. When they came to the end, Kathrine felt like going another five miles. So, she finished at thirty-one miles. Arnie stayed with her, but he passed out at the end.

Now Kathrine knew she could run a marathon—the 1967 Boston Marathon. But no women were allowed. She filled out her application as "K.V. Switzer" so the marathon organizers wouldn't know she was a woman, and her application was accepted.

The day of the race, she put on her baggy sweatpants and lined up with her number pinned on her sweatshirt. Kathrine's boyfriend, an All-American football player and nationally ranked hammer thrower, Tom Miller, decided to race with her. He thought that if a woman could run a marathon, he could too—without training.

After they had raced a few miles, one of the officials riding with the film crew noticed that Kathrine was a woman and tried to rip her number off her and push her out of the race. Women were not allowed in the Boston Marathon, he said. Kathrine's boyfriend shoved the official to the side of the road, and Kathrine kept running. The camera crew caught the entire incident on film.

Kathrine and her coach, Arnie, finished the race, and Tom came limping in a little later. (He found out it was tough to run a marathon without training.) On the way back to Syracuse that evening, they stopped to get gas and saw a newspaper with Kathrine's picture. People all over the country were thrilled that Kathrine had run and finished the race. Soon, the American Athletic Union (AAU) had to admit women runners.

In 1974, she was the women's winner of the New York City Marathon. She was named the Female Runner of the Decade (1967-1977) for *Runner's World Magazine*.

Because of Kathrine's confidence, fitness, and hard work, she changed women's sports forever. Now women participate in athletic events all over the world.

YOU CAN BE A HERO	Kathrine loved exercise and working hard. What do you like to do? If you work hard at it, you will accomplish your goals just like Kathrine did.

"I REALIZE THAT THAT BLANK PAGE IS A MAGIC BOX. . . . IT NEEDS TO BE FILLED WITH SOMETHING FANTASTIC."

—J. J. ABRAMS

J. J. ABRAMS

1966–

SPECIAL POWERS:	CREATIVITY

Jeffrey Jacobs Abrams used his imagination to create magic from the time he was little. He grew up in Pacific Palisades, California, where both his parents were television producers. He remembers sitting in his crib, reading books and discovering the magic of stories. His teacher in grade school thought he should be playing dodge ball with the other kids, but J. J. loved running around the schoolyard with a red cape on, making up stories.

J. J. and his grandfather loved to do magic tricks together. But J. J. could see other kinds of magic all around him—in every story he thought up, in the movies he saw, and in the films he crafted. Since his parents were television producers, he grew up watching shows like *Happy Days* and *Laverne and Shirley* as they were being filmed. To him, they became magic on the television.

As a teenager, he got a Super 8 camera and began making 8 mm movies (8 mm was the width of the film used in the camera). At age fifteen, he produced a film called *High Voltage* and was interviewed by the *Los Angeles Times*. Steven Spielberg—the famous director of *Jaws*, *E.T.*, and *Jurassic Park*—read the newspaper article and asked J. J. if he would repair Spielberg's old 8 mm films. J. J. was very excited. When he went through Spielberg's early attempts at filmmaking, J. J. realized that everyone—even Spielberg—had to practice and work hard to learn how to make film magic.

After high school, J. J. went to Sarah Lawrence College outside New York City and learned everything he could about good entertainment. He went on to write magical stories for movies, television shows, video games, and musical soundtracks. His works include *Star Wars: Episode VII*, *Star Trek*, *Mission: Impossible III*, *Joy Ride*, *Armageddon*, *Gone Fishing*, *Regarding Henry*, and *Super 8* with many more yet to come. He also created the Lost and Alias series for television.

Science fiction fans didn't think he could direct both the Star Trek and Star Wars movies. They said they were different kinds of magic. J. J. worried that maybe the fans were right. Perhaps they really were too different. But he talked with his wife, and she encouraged him to do both if he wanted to. He did— and produced two magic hits.

J. J. used his creativity to build new worlds, create entertainment, and inspire others with powerful stories. And when all is said and done, that's the greatest magic of all.

YOU CAN BE A HERO	Stories were magic to J. J. What is magic to you? How can you create magic for others?

"IF YOU WANT TO LIFT
YOURSELF UP, LIFT UP
SOMEONE ELSE."
—BOOKER T. WASHINGTON

BOOKER T. WASHINGTON

1856–1915

SPECIAL POWERS:	LEADERSHIP	EDUCATION

Booker was born a slave in Virginia. He and his older brother, John, worked in the cotton fields and tended the animals with the master's children. Booker's mother, Jane, cooked for the family. After the Civil War, Booker's stepfather, Washington, moved the family to Malden, West Virginia, and John and Booker worked in the coal mines. Booker really wanted to go to school. His mother bought him a Webster's spelling book, which he studied every evening. There was a night school in Tinkersville, and Booker went so he could learn. When the teacher asked him his full name, he didn't know it. He thought fast and answered, "Booker Washington," after his stepfather. His mother later told him his middle name was Taliaferro, so he called himself Booker T. Washington.

He heard of a school called Hampton Institute in Virginia. He was determined to go there and continue his education. He worked and saved until he thought he had enough money to get there, but he had to walk the last eighty miles. When he got to the school, he was tired, ragged, and dirty. He asked the principal if he could work to pay his way. She asked him to clean the recitation room. He scrubbed and dusted and polished the room until it shone. She accepted Booker because she knew he would be a hard worker.

Booker got along well with the teachers and other students. He graduated and was recommended to open the Tuskegee Institute in Alabama so other African Americans could go to school. When he got to Tuskegee, there was no land or buildings or books. Booker opened the school anyway in a shanty behind one of the churches with thirty students. He wrote to the Hampton Institute to send him any supplies they could.

He soon came up with enough money to buy some land. The students had to grow their own food. They also learned to make bricks so they could build their own buildings.

Booker's school was a great success because of his leadership (it's a university with almost 3,000 students today). He spoke all over the country and asked people to donate money. Booker became friends with Andrew Carnegie and John D. Rockefeller, two of the richest men in the United States at the time, and they also helped support his school. He even dined at the White House with President Theodore Roosevelt.

Booker thought that African Americans should get along with whites the best they could. He spoke about peace between the groups. African Americans liked his ideas of brotherhood at first, but toward the end of Booker's life, they wanted equality—not just peace. A new generation of leaders like Martin Luther King Jr. fought to win that equality for all people. Today, Booker's ideas of humanity and peace are still important—along with equality. His leadership and love of education inspired change for millions of people.

YOU CAN BE A HERO	Booker wanted people to get along and live peacefully together. Are you a peacemaker? How can you get along with those around you?

"MAKE EACH DAY YOUR
MASTERPIECE."
–JOHN WOODEN

JOHN WOODEN

1910–2010

SPECIAL POWERS:	FITNESS	FAMILY	LEADERSHIP

John grew up in Indiana—basketball country. He and his three brothers played basketball all year round in their barn. He lived on a farm, so he learned to work hard.

As the star basketball player, he led the Martinsville High School team to the state championship in 1927. He went on to college at Purdue where he was an All-American player for three years and voted the College Basketball Player of the Year for 1932. He also graduated with honors in English.

John served in the navy during World War II. When he returned home, Indiana State Teacher's College hired him as their basketball coach. He trained his team to work hard, and they won two conference titles. After that, University of California at Los Angeles (UCLA) and University of Minnesota (U of M) both wanted him as their coach. Because of bad weather, John didn't receive the phone call offer from the U of M, so he took the job at UCLA.

When John met the players, he found them swearing and criticizing each other. He made them stop immediately—no cursing and no backbiting. The team began to play together and won three conference titles in the next few years.

In 1963-64, John's UCLA team won all thirty of their games and the national championship. He was named Coach of the Year. His team later went on to win seven straight national championships.

John was inducted into the Basketball Hall of Fame. He was the first person to be both an All-American player and a Hall-of-Fame coach. But John's true love in life was something much more than basketball. Her name was Nellie.

Nellie Riley was the love of John's life. They had known each other since high school and were married when John returned from World War II. When Nellie died of cancer in 1985, she and John had been married for fifty-three years. Then, every month for the next twenty-five years after his wife's death, John visited her crypt in the mausoleum and wrote her a love letter. He piled the letters on the pillow of her bed.

Yes, John received lots of honors in his life. Many schools were named after him. President George W. Bush presented him with the Presidential Medal of Freedom, the nation's highest civilian honor. A statue of John was dedicated at the new Pauley Pavilion (the sports arena on UCLA campus) in Los Angeles, California. But John's greatest legacy was a life lived in love and friendship. He taught his players—and the world—to work hard, be kind, and let your goodness shine.

YOU CAN BE A HERO	John loved his family. He wrote letters to his wife, telling her how much he loved her. What could you do to show someone you loved them?

CORRIE TEN BOOM

1892–1983

SPECIAL POWERS:	FORGIVENESS	COURAGE

Corrie grew up as the youngest in her family. Her father was a watchmaker and a jeweler. Corrie loved working with her father, and in 1922, she became the first woman in the Netherlands licensed as a watchmaker. Corrie's home in Amsterdam was a hub of activity. The family had many friends and loved helping people in need. Corrie began a youth club for teenage girls where they learned the performing arts, held religious study, and practiced sewing.

When the Nazis invaded the Netherlands in 1940, Corrie had to quit holding classes. The Nazis also wanted to round up the Jews, so Corrie and her sister, Betsie, began hiding Jews and became part of the underground. Resistance members hid building materials in large grandfather clocks and carried them up the steep stairs to Corrie's room. There, they built a secret hiding place where the Jews could go when the Nazis raided the house. Corrie had the Jews practice so they could get into the secret room very quickly—in just one minute.

Corrie and her family rescued over 800 Jews and many Dutch resistance fighters. But in 1944, Corrie and her family were betrayed by an informant, arrested, and sent to concentration camps. Corrie and Betsie ended up at the Ravensbrück concentration camp in Germany. Corrie managed to smuggle in a copy of the New Testament without the guards noticing. She and other prisoners held a church service every evening. Their barracks became infested with fleas, but it turned out to be a good thing—the guards left their barracks alone. Corrie said the fleas were a blessing because they could worship as they wished without being disturbed. Prisoners of many different religions read the New Testament together. Corrie or Betsie would read a scripture passage in Dutch, and the women would pass the message along in French, Polish, Russian, German, and Czech. Corrie said these meetings were like a little glimpse into heaven.

Betsie died in the concentration camp just a short time before the war ended. Corrie was released from the camp because of a clerical error. She called it a miracle because several days later, many women her age died.

After the war, Corrie went back to the Netherlands and established a home to rehabilitate concentration camp survivors. She even helped the Dutch people who were Nazi sympathizers. Several years later, she returned to Germany to meet and forgive the two guards who had been cruel to her in Ravensbrück. From there, she began to give speeches all over the world about love and forgiveness.

In 1971, she wrote a book called *The Hiding Place* in which she talked about her experiences during the war. The book was made into a movie. She was honored by the State of Israel as "Righteous Among Nations" and she was knighted by the Queen of the Netherlands. Her courage saved the lives of hundreds during the war, and her example of forgiveness impacted many more afterwards.

YOU CAN BE A HERO	Corrie forgave the guards who were mean to her. What can you do to show others you forgive them?

"CHARACTER IS MOST DETERMINED BY INTEGRITY AND COURAGE."
—JON HUNTSMAN SR.

JON HUNTSMAN SR.

1937–2018

SPECIAL POWERS:	INTEGRITY	COMPASSION	HARD WORK

Jon Huntsman Sr. grew up in Blackfoot, Idaho, where his father was a teacher. The family was poor. At first they didn't even have indoor plumbing. In 1950, his father wanted to go to school at Stanford University, so he moved the family to Palo Alto, California. At junior high school, Jon met his future wife, Karen, and they became good friends. Jon loved people and got along with everyone. The kids voted him student body president of the high school.

After high school, he received a scholarship to attend the Wharton School of Business in Philadelphia, Pennsylvania. It was one of the best business schools in the country. John wanted to be successful because he always remembered being poor. He worked hard on his studies. After graduating from college, he worked for a California company that manufactured polystyrene plastics.

Soon, he started his own plastics business and made lots of products. On the side, he took a job as staff secretary to President Richard Nixon. He stayed on as part of the White House staff for a little while and then left to take care of his businesses.

Jon worked hard to build his business. He bought quite a few plastics companies around the world. One of them was the Texaco Chemical company. At that time, many people disliked the company and said Texaco didn't treat their employees very well. When Jon purchased the company, he told Mr. Reaud, one of the lawyers who disliked Texaco also, to give him a chance; he would treat the employees better than the others had. Jon kept his word, and Mr. Reaud later said that Jon was "the greatest man I know."

Jon was known for his integrity and was famous for his handshake deals. If he said he would do something, that was as good as a contract. Once, he promised to sell part of his business to someone for $53 million. Time passed before the sale happened, and during that time, the value of the business increased to over $200 million. Because the deal wasn't final yet, Jon could have raised the price to over $200 million instead—but he didn't. "A deal is a deal. A handshake is a handshake. Integrity is integrity," he later said. He lost out on nearly $200 million, but he kept his integrity. That was worth more to him than any amount of money.

Over the years, Jon did make lots of money. When a group of other rich men pledged half their money to charity, John thought it would be better to give away even more. He donated to universities, religious charities, and homeless communities. He created the Huntsman Cancer Center in Salt Lake City, Utah, because both his parents died of cancer. Over his lifetime, he donated almost $2 billion to make the world a better place.

Jon's kindness and integrity became known throughout the world of business. He showed others that you didn't have to be dishonest to be successful. Good, honest, hard work was enough. And as for generosity, that had its own reward—one even greater.

YOU CAN BE A HERO	Jon was honest in his dealings with others. He always told the truth. His word was his bond. Are you honest with those around you? If you say you'll do something, be sure you do it.

CAESAR RODNEY

SPECIAL POWERS:	COURAGE	INDEPENDENCE

Caesar Rodney loved America and loved freedom. He grew up the oldest of eight children in Delaware, one of the British colonies in America. His father died when he was young, so he had to help raise his brothers and sisters and take care of the large family farm.

The people trusted him and voted him sheriff of Kent County, Delaware. After this three-year term, he served in other offices, including the Delaware legislature. Everyone respected him, so he was appointed to the Delaware Supreme Court—and he wasn't even a lawyer.

Caesar had asthma, and his health wasn't very good. He had cancer on his face, and the doctors cut it out, leaving a big gash. He was embarrassed about it and tried to cover it with a scarf.

Many Americans living in the colonies felt they were being treated unfairly by the British government. In 1774, a group of representatives from each colony met to decide what to do. This was called the First Continental Congress. Delaware selected Caesar as their representative, along with Thomas McKean and George Read. Months went by, and Congress debated whether they should try to be free from England. Caesar and Thomas McKean wanted America to be free, but George Read was loyal to England.

Eventually, Congress called for a vote to see if the delegates wanted to remain loyal to England or declare their independence. Caesar was home in Delaware at the time taking care of some unruly soldiers. Thomas McKean sent a messenger to Caesar to come immediately so they could vote for freedom against George Read. Without Caesar's vote, there would be a tie and those who wanted freedom wouldn't win.

Despite his poor health, Caesar saddled up his horse and rode like Paul Revere all night in the rain—eighty miles in fourteen hours. He was muddy and wet when he got to Philadelphia where Congress met, but he was just in time to vote for freedom. July 4th became the birthday of America, and on August 2, 1776, Caesar and most of the other delegates signed the Declaration of Independence. If Caesar hadn't risked his health to make it in time, the vote for freedom might never have passed.

Caesar continued to fight for freedom during the Revolutionary War. His best friend, John Haslet, was a colonel in the 1st Delaware Regiment. When Caesar heard that John had been killed in battle, Caesar raced to take John's place in the fight. Caesar was later the major general of the Delaware militia and fought with George Washington. After the war, Caesar served in the state legislature and as governor of Delaware from 1778-1781. His cancer came back, and at times he was so ill that the assembly came to his home to meet because Caesar couldn't travel.

Caesar Rodney voted for freedom, signed for freedom, and fought for freedom. A statue of him astride a horse can be seen in Rodney Square in Wilmington, Delaware, as a tribute to his service to his country. His courage and patriotism gave birth to a new nation and inspired its citizens to this day.

YOU CAN BE A HERO	Caesar loved freedom, so he served his country in lots of ways. What can you do to serve your country?

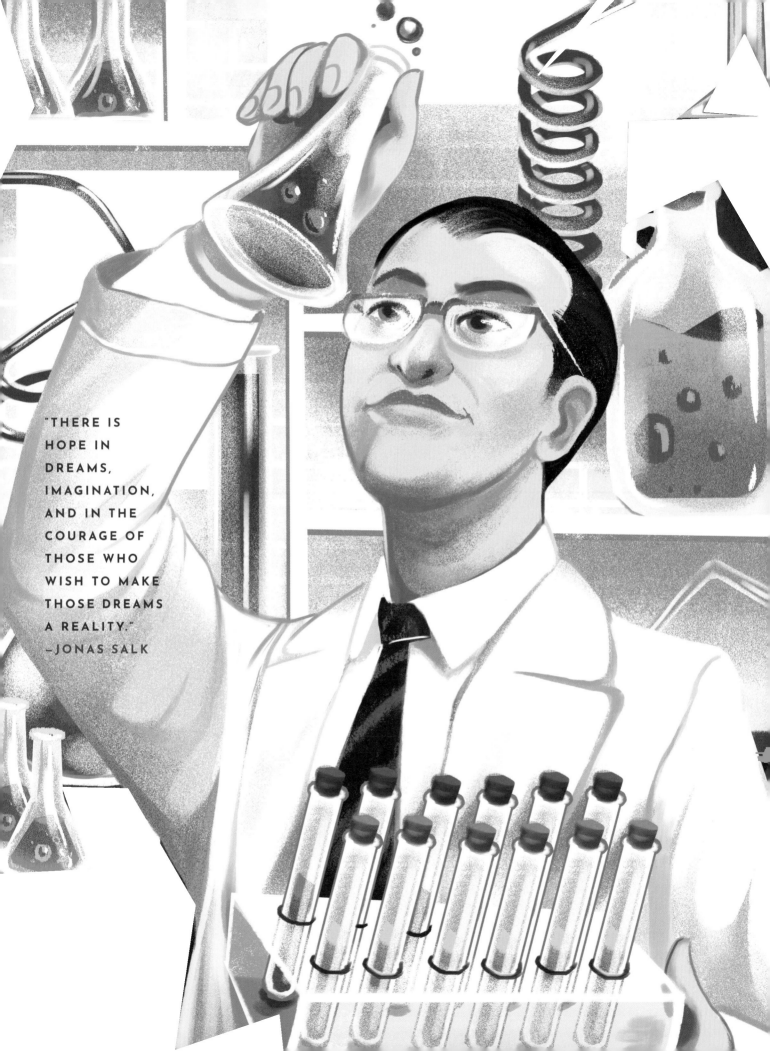

"THERE IS HOPE IN DREAMS, IMAGINATION, AND IN THE COURAGE OF THOSE WHO WISH TO MAKE THOSE DREAMS A REALITY."
—JONAS SALK

JONAS SALK

1914–1995

SPECIAL POWERS:	EDUCATION	COMPASSION

Jonas Salk was born in New York City when the disease of polio was spreading in epidemic proportions throughout the city. Polio attacked the nerves of children so that they couldn't walk or run. They were confined to wheelchairs. When Jonas was two, his family moved out of the city to the Bronx where they thought it was safer. They didn't want Jonas to get polio.

Fortunately, Jonas didn't get the disease, and at only age twelve, he was ready for high school—a gifted high school where he graduated in just three years. At age fifteen, he entered the City College of New York. His parents didn't have enough money to pay for his college, but he got a scholarship. He thought about studying law, but he loved microbiology—the study of bacteria and viruses.

In 1940, at the time of World War II, Jonas worked in a lab to develop a flu vaccine so soldiers wouldn't get sick. After the war, he studied the immune system—how to keep people well. But most of all, Jonas wanted to help fight polio.

At that time, Franklin Delano Roosevelt was president of the United States. He got polio when he was thirty-nine and couldn't walk. Roosevelt helped start the March of Dimes and asked everyone to send money to support polio research. The people of the United States sent $3 million to President Roosevelt, and Jonas used the money to work on a vaccine that would prevent polio.

In 1954, Jonas believed he had succeeded. The vaccine was ready to give to boys and girls, but Jonas was worried. He said he didn't sleep well at night for several weeks, hoping that the vaccine wouldn't hurt the children. He even gave himself and his family the vaccine to make sure it was safe.

But Jonas had done his research and his medicine was a huge success. People from all over the country wanted their children to have the vaccine so they wouldn't get polio. The doctors said the medicine was "safe, effective, and potent." Before the vaccine, there were at least 25,000 cases of polio each year and sometimes as many as 50,000. But three years after the vaccine, there were less than 6,000 cases. Today, the World Health Organization says that polio will soon be gone worldwide.

Jonas never took any money for himself from the vaccine. He didn't get a patent, either. He said the vaccine belonged to everyone.

Jonas didn't stop with polio. Researchers helped him build the Salk Institute for Biological Studies where Jonas began research on an AIDS vaccine. In 1977, he received the Presidential Medal of Freedom from President Jimmy Carter.

Jonas spent his life learning and researching so other people could stay well. Today, many people around the world enjoy good health, free from a crippling disease.

YOU CAN BE A HERO	Jonas didn't want children to be sick. He worked hard to make them well. How can you keep yourself healthy? What can you do to help those around you stay well?

"THE END OF ALL
KNOWLEDGE SHOULD BE
SERVICE TO OTHERS."
–CÉSAR CHÁVEZ

CÉSAR CHÁVEZ

1927–1993

SPECIAL POWERS:	LEADERSHIP	COURAGE	JUSTICE

César Chavéz began his life in Yuma, Arizona, where his family owned a grocery store and a vegetable farm. They lost the farm during the Great Depression and moved to California to become migrant workers. They picked beans, cherries, and lettuce in the spring; grapes, tomatoes, and corn in the summer; and cotton in the fall.

When he wasn't working in the fields, César attended school. Because his family moved with the harvest, he attended many schools for a short time—sixty-five in all. Sometimes the teachers hit him because he spoke Spanish. He felt sad because he loved his language.

When César was fifteen, his father got hurt, so César quit school and worked full time to support his family. He kept reading to educate himself, and when he grew older, he acquired a large library.

During World War II, he served in the navy for two years. When the war was over, César met and married Helen Fabela. They lived in San Jose, California, and had eight children.

A man named Fred Ross from the Community Service Organization (CSO) talked to César about registering to vote. He told César that poor people needed to speak out. César listened. He was shy at first, but soon he became confident and urged all the farmworkers to register to vote.

César also worked to make sure farmworkers were treated fairly. At the time, grape pickers only earned one dollar per hour. César started the United Farm Workers Organizing Committee (UFWOC) to fight for better pay. In order to get the farmers to listen, César went without eating to bring attention to the unfair treatment of the grape pickers. It worked, and the farmers began to pay the workers more money. In honor of César's achievement, Senator Robert F. Kennedy flew across the country to give César his first piece of bread to break his fast.

A few years later, César fasted again to draw attention to the illnesses pickers got from the dangerous chemicals farmers sprayed on the grapes. He helped bring about changes in the use of harmful chemicals.

César died in his sleep in 1993 at the home of a friend in Arizona. The next year, President Bill Clinton gave Helen Chavéz, César's wife, the Presidential Medal of Freedom for his hard work on behalf of the farmworkers. He was inducted into the California Hall of Fame. His birthday, March 31, is César Chavéz day in California, Colorado, and Texas.

César dedicated his life to make things better and more just for all people. Through his leadership and courage, he did just that.

YOU CAN BE A HERO	César gave a voice to those who struggled to be heard. Do you know people whose needs get overlooked? How could you help them have a voice?

"EXTEND A SINGLE ACT OF KINDNESS, A TOKEN OF MERCY, OR AN EXPRESSION OF FORGIVENESS."
—CHRIS WILLIAMS

CHRIS WILLIAMS

SPECIAL POWERS:	FORGIVENESS	FAMILY	FRIENDSHIP

Chris Williams and his wife and children were traveling home one evening when their car was broadsided by a teenage driver. He heard the crunch of metal and felt the shock of the impact. He felt stunned. Pain rocketed through his leg when he tried to move it, and he knew it was damaged. He turned his head and looked at his wife, Michelle. She wasn't breathing. He glanced in the back seat at his son, Ben (age 11), and his daughter, Anna (age 9). They had died, too. He couldn't turn to see Sam (age 6), but he heard him cry out in pain.

That moment felt unreal to Chris. This couldn't be happening. Dazed, he looked out the window at the car that had hit them. He closed his eyes and heard a voice as if someone were sitting next to him. The voice said, "Let it go." Chris was filled with a sense of peace.

The driver of that car was Cameron, a seventeen-year-old who had been drinking. In the hospital, Chris asked a friend to check on Cameron. Chris wanted to make sure he was all right. As Chris lay in the hospital, he could feel love for that boy. Chris prayed for Cameron.

A few days later, Chris met with the news media. He asked everyone to perform an act of kindness to show forgiveness for Cameron—a gift to Michelle, Ben, and Anna. People could write about their service experience and send it to Chris and his family. As he spoke at the news conference, he felt thousands of hands supporting him in his time of trial.

Chris was lonely without his wife and children. He prayed that he could find happiness in his life again. As he thought about the accident, he knew he hadn't lost his family forever. He believed he would be with Michelle and his children again in heaven. So Chris began to serve others.

During Cameron's trial, Chris asked Cameron to make something of his life as a tribute to his Michelle, Ben, and Anna.

There are many kinds of strength in this world. Chris's love for his family gave him strength to move forward. His love for Cameron gave him strength to become a friend. Then, Chris showed one of the greatest strengths of all: he chose to forgive.

YOU CAN BE A HERO	Chris forgave Cameron and tried to make sure he was okay. He didn't want to be angry inside. He wanted to feel love and peace. What can you do to keep love and peace in your life? Is there someone you feel you could forgive?

"NOTHING IN LIFE
IS TO BE FEARED—
IT IS ONLY TO BE
UNDERSTOOD. NOW
IS THE TIME TO
UNDERSTAND MORE,
SO THAT WE MAY
FEAR LESS."
—MARIE CURIE

MARIE CURIE

1867–1934

SPECIAL POWERS:	INTELLIGENCE	COMPASSION

One of Maria Skłodowska's earliest memories was of being fascinated by the scientific instruments in her father's cabinet. She taught herself to read when she was only four.

In Warsaw, Poland, where she grew up, the Russians occupied the country. The school officials and teachers were angry if anyone spoke Polish, so Maria was very careful to speak only Russian. But she loved learning—especially reading her father's physics books.

Maria was devastated when her older sister died of typhoid fever and her mother died of tuberculosis. She took over many of the household duties as she grew up. Girls in Poland weren't allowed to go to college, so Maria and her older sister, Bronya, decided to help each other get an education. Maria worked as a governess while Bronya studied in Paris, France, and then Bronya helped Maria go to school. When Maria first got to Paris, she changed her name to Marie and studied extra hard to remember her French so she could do well in school. She caught up in her studies and graduated first in her class in physics and got a second degree in mathematics. At Sorbonne University, she met Pierre Curie, another physicist. They fell in love and were married.

Marie continued to study and do research. She began to investigate the invisible energy in the elements uranium and thorium. She knew that pitchblende, a black ore, contained both ingredients, so she got several tons of it and went to work. Pierre joined her in her research, and they isolated radioactive energy in polonium and radium (mineral elements discovered by Marie). Their laboratory was in an old building. A visiting scientist called it a "cross between a stable and a potato-cellar." But Marie and Pierre didn't care. They loved being together and doing their research.

In 1903, the Curies received the Nobel Prize in physics. Marie was the first woman to receive this award. But three years later, Pierre was killed by a heavy horse cart when he stepped off the curb on a busy Paris street. Marie was grief-stricken. There was no one to teach Pierre's classes at Sorbonne University, so Marie taught them. She was the first woman to teach at the university. She continued her research and received a second Nobel Prize in 1911 for chemistry—the first person to receive a Nobel Prize twice.

But Marie's incredible work didn't happen only in a laboratory. During World War I, she wanted to help defend her country. She put her research on hold and set to work designing mobile X-ray units that could be driven to the frontlines of battle to help treat wounded soldiers. She drove one of the cars herself, helping to examine soldiers for bullets and broken bones. She set up X-rays in field hospitals, too. Marie even tried to melt her golden Nobel Prize medals so she could help fund the war effort. Through her efforts, more than one million soldiers were helped during the war.

Women everywhere revere Marie for her pioneering work in science at a time that women weren't allowed. Now, many women follow in her intelligent, compassionate footsteps to make the world a better place through scientific exploration.

YOU CAN BE A HERO	Marie loved learning. She wanted to know more about the world. What do you want to know more about? How can you learn about it? Could you share what you learn with others like Marie did?

"I THINK WE HAVE TO TEACH A LOT OF THESE KIDS TO FIRST BE GENTLEMEN, [TO] TRY TO HELP ONE ANOTHER AND NOT HOG THE DOGGONE WAVES."
—DUKE KAHANAMOKU

DUKE KAHANAMOKU

1890–1968

SPECIAL POWERS:	FITNESS

When Duke Kahanamoku was four years old, his father threw him over the side of a boat and told him to swim. Duke did. He became such a good swimmer that people called him a human fish.

There were no swimming pools in Hawaii at that time, so Duke swam in Honolulu Harbor. In 1911, he shattered the world swimming record for the hundred-yard freestyle by four seconds. He also broke the fifty-yard freestyle record. The American Athletic Union (AAU) didn't believe Duke really swam that fast. They said the timers must have used alarm clocks instead of stopwatches. They hadn't. Duke didn't get credit for his times until later.

In 1912, Duke won a gold medal in the Olympics for the hundred-meter freestyle and a silver medal in the 4x200-meter freestyle relay. In the 1920 Olympics, he won a gold medal in the hundred-meter freestyle again and the relay got gold also. In the 1924 Olympics, the United States swept the medals for the hundred-meter freestyle. Johnny Weissmuller took gold, Duke received silver, and Duke's little brother, Sam, got bronze.

But there was one thing Duke loved even more than swimming: surfing. His favorite beach in Hawaii was Waikiki. He wanted surfing to be an Olympic sport, but no one knew anything about it. It had only been an old Hawaiian sport, so Duke decided to teach people about it. He taught in Australia, Southern California, and gave demonstrations in Atlantic City, New Jersey—riding his board backwards, and then standing on his head, and then carrying a boy on his shoulders. Everyone loved Duke and his surfing, and in time, the sport became popular. Today, Duke is called the father of modern surfing.

In 1925, Duke saw a fishing boat capsize in the water off Newport Beach. He could see from the shore that the men were in trouble. He paddled out into the surf and brought some of the men back with him on his board. His friends also helped, saving four others. The police chief honored him, and because of Duke, many lifeguards in Southern California still use rescue boards to this day.

Duke acted in small parts in movies in Southern California. Sometimes people treated him badly because he had brown skin. Duke knew it was unfair, but he decided to be kind back instead.

Eventually, Duke and his wife went back to Hawaii where he served as sheriff of Honolulu from 1934 to 1961. When he retired, the city asked him to greet famous people that came to Hawaii, including Babe Ruth and President John F. Kennedy. The United States Postal Service even issued a stamp in his honor.

Duke used his athletic gift to bring honor to his country, invent a new sport, and even save lives.

YOU CAN BE A HERO	Duke loved surfing and swimming, but he also loved people. He combined his love of sports with his love of people and was able to help both. What do you love? How could that help people?

"EDUCATION IS
WHAT ALLOWS YOU
TO STAND OUT."
—ELLEN OCHOA

ELLEN OCHOA

NASA

ELLEN OCHOA

1958–

SPECIAL POWERS:	HARD WORK	EDUCATION

When Ellen began to play the flute as a little girl, she didn't know she would one day be the first person to play the flute in space.

Ellen was born in Los Angeles, California, as one of five children. Ellen loved learning, just like her mother, Rosanne, who worked to support the family and went to college herself. (Rosanne kept going to school until she earned three different degrees in twenty-two years!)

Ellen loved math, science, and music. She played the flute in her orchestra. She worked hard in school and was top of her graduating class.

After high school, Ellen received a scholarship to attend Stanford University, but she decided to go to San Diego State University to be near her brothers. She was interested in many subjects and changed her major several times, studying journalism, business, computer science, and finally physics. She graduated top of her class again and went on to receive her PhD from Stanford University.

Ellen didn't think about becoming an astronaut until some of her friends applied to become one. She realized that she had the qualifications, so she sent an application to NASA's astronaut program. She was very excited when she was accepted. In 1990, she began training at the Johnson Space Center in Houston, Texas. She became the first Latino woman to fly into space.

Practicing to become an astronaut was difficult. She had to train for anything that might go wrong. She learned to parachute, survive in the water, and subsist in the wilderness. The trainees also had to practice weightlessness. They flew in a jet very high, and when the jet dropped straight down for almost two miles, the astronauts became weightless. They did this forty times in three hours. They called the jet the "Vomit Comet."

Ellen flew with the Discovery mission in 1993, the Atlantis mission in 1994, and the Atlantis again in 2002. Her job was to control a robotic arm that had a wrist, elbow, and shoulder. She used a hand controller that looked something like a joystick. On the Discovery mission, she used the arm to launch a satellite from the shuttle and hook it back again. On the Atlantis mission, she used the arm to move the astronauts around to do their work.

After she retired as an astronaut in 2012, Ellen became the director of the Johnson Space Center. Several schools around the United States have been named after her. She also received NASA's Exceptional Service Medal, Outstanding Leadership Medal, and has been inducted into the United States Astronaut Hall of Fame.

Ellen loves being a role model for girls today. When she was young, there weren't many people cheering girls on to become whatever they wanted to be. Now Ellen enjoys speaking to youth everywhere, reminding them to use their education and hard work to reach for the stars—just like she did.

YOU CAN BE A HERO	Ellen couldn't decide what her dreams were when she was young. But as she grew older, she knew. Now she encourages young people to reach for their dreams. What do you dream about becoming? What can you do today to reach for those goals?

YASUTERU YAMADA

1939–

SPECIAL POWERS:	COMPASSION	SACRIFICE	FAMILY

Yasuteru Yamada lived in Japan all his life. He was now an old man and a retired engineer. But when a tsunami hit Japan in 2011, Yamada decided it was time to leave retirement—his country needed him.

When the tsunami and earthquake struck, a nuclear power plant in Fukushima was severely damaged. Radiation was leaking and it was very dangerous. The Tepco Company running the plant needed workers to bring the plant to a complete shutdown. Yasuteru Yamada talked to his friend, Nobuhiro Shiotani, and they decided they could help.

Yamada and Shiotani knew that radiation was harmful and could cause cancer. They felt it was much better for older people to be exposed to radiation than younger ones. They said they would not live long enough to develop cancer like the younger people would. They were worried about what would happen to the younger workers and their families.

What could they do? Yamada and Shiotani contacted their retired friends and asked if they would help them take care of the radiation leaks. Their friends responded immediately. About 500 volunteers signed up, some as old as eighty-two. Donations poured in too—about $100,000. Yamada organized the Skilled Veterans Corps made up of retired engineers and other older professionals to go to work.

He met the Japanese Minister of Economy, Trade, and Industry to get permission to help. The Skilled Veterans Corps stood by, waiting for approval. They didn't want any money. They just wanted to work hard and protect the younger workers and their families.

Today, Yamada and Shiotani are still waiting. The Tepco Company is grateful for the retirees' offer, and they are still deciding if the older people can do the work. The company wants to ensure the retirees' safety.

Meanwhile, Yamada and Shiotani have been so busy, they rented a small office where they have two computers, some folding chairs, and a hot water pot. One news report said the office looked like they could have been planning a neighborhood senior breakfast, but of course, they were really preparing to clean up a nuclear disaster.

When tragedy struck, Yamada showed the world what quiet sacrifice could do. It's true that earthquakes may still strike. Tsunamis may still hit. Hurricanes and tornadoes may still destroy. But compassion like that of Yamada—and of those who volunteered alongside him—is more powerful than anything.

YOU CAN BE A HERO	Yamada was willing to do something dangerous so others could be safe—a sacrifice. Have you ever given up something you wanted so someone else could have it? How did it make you feel? How do you think it made the other person feel? Look for more opportunities to show genuine love by sacrificing for those you care about.

"I WENT INTO TELEVISION BECAUSE I HATED IT SO, AND I THOUGHT THERE WAS SOME WAY OF USING THIS FABULOUS INSTRUMENT TO NURTURE THOSE WHO WOULD WATCH AND LISTEN."

—FRED ROGERS

FRED ROGERS

1928–2003

SPECIAL POWERS:	COMPASSION	CREATIVITY

F red loved people—especially children. He always put on his sweater and sang, "Won't you be my neighbor?" at the beginning of his television show, *Mister Rogers' Neighborhood*. At the end of his show, he took off his sweater, hung it in the closet, and told the children, "I like you just the way you are."

It took a lot of confidence to host a national television show that was so different from the other shows for children. But Fred wasn't always so self-assured. As a child, he was shy and sickly. He was overweight, and kids called him "Fat Freddy." He spent most of his time in his bedroom playing with his puppets and stuffed animals and making up stories. But when he got to high school, he overcame his shyness. He made a couple of friends—one of them was head of the football team. He was elected president of the student council and became a member of the National Honor Society. He graduated from college with a degree in music.

His television career began with a show called *The Children's Hour* in 1953 where Fred helped create the puppets and the music. Then, the Canadian Broadcasting Company asked him to do a children's program called *Misterogers*. He later came back to the United States and started *Mister Rogers' Neighborhood*, which began in 1968.

During the show, Fred talked directly to the children who were watching from home. Sometimes he went on a field trip to visit a bakery or to see a bulldozer. And of course, there was always a visit to the Neighborhood of Make-Believe with his famous trolley. Fred spoke to issues of the day and about kindness and acceptance. Once, when parts of America still had separate schools for white and black children, he and François Clemmons, an African American, had a footbath together on the show. They showed that people with different colored skin could be friends and shouldn't be afraid of each other.

Fred's programs were quiet and gentle, unlike the fast-paced, frantic children's comedies of the day. He loved children, and children loved him because of his peaceful, unhurried messages.

One day, Fred appeared before a congressional subcommittee to testify on behalf of the Public Broadcasting System (PBS). He told Congress about all the good public television did. The committee chairman, Senator John O. Pastore, was so impressed with Fred's testimony that he increased PBS funding from $9 million to $22 million.

Fred won four Emmy Awards and a Lifetime Achievement Award in daytime television. He received many other honors, including the Presidential Medal of Freedom bestowed on him by President George Bush.

His compassion and creativity added goodness and light to the lives of an entire generation of children who will remember him as a happy part of their childhood.

YOU CAN BE A HERO	Mr. Rogers used his talents to bring light and love to the world. How can you use your talents to show others that you care?

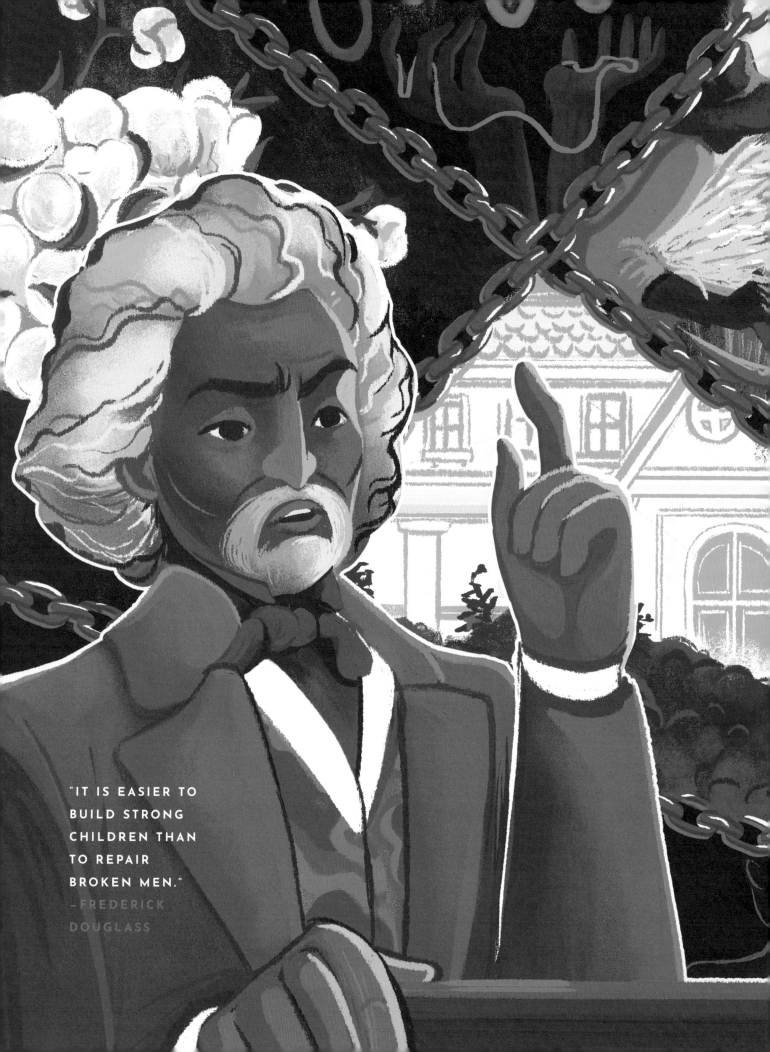

"IT IS EASIER TO BUILD STRONG CHILDREN THAN TO REPAIR BROKEN MEN."
—FREDERICK DOUGLASS

FREDERICK DOUGLASS

1817–1895

SPECIAL POWERS:	JUSTICE	INDEPENDENCE

Frederick was born a slave in Maryland. At first, his grandmother Betsey took care of him. But when Frederick was six, Betsey took him on a long walk to a big house and left him. He never saw her again.

At this new house, Frederick and the other children were fed cornmeal mush in a trough in the yard—just like pigs. They never had spoons. They scooped the mush with bits of shell or pieces of wood. A slave named Aunt Katy took care of the children. She disliked Frederick, and when she was angry with him, she made him go hungry.

When he was eight, he went to Baltimore to work for the Hugh and Sophia Auld family. His job was to care for their son, two-year-old Tommy. Sophia loved to read the Bible to the boys. Inspired by her reading, Frederick asked Sophia to teach him to read, too. She did, and Frederick not only learned to read, but also how to speak like Sophia. Hugh was angry with Sophia for teaching Frederick. Hugh said that if slaves could read, they would run away. When Frederick heard this, he studied even harder.

As he grew older, he worked at the shipyards. Frederick watched the ships and remembered which ones sailed north, always searching for a way to be free. Baltimore was close to the Northern states, and that meant close to freedom.

Sometimes, slave owners traded slaves around. Hugh sent Frederick to Edward Covey, who lived farther south. Edward Covey beat Frederick over and over. Finally, Frederick had enough and fought back. Edward couldn't control Frederick, so he sent him back to Hugh Auld.

Frederick was back in Baltimore—nearer to the free states. Now was Frederick's chance to escape. He put on a sailor's uniform, hopped on a train north, and ended up in New York City.

He settled in Boston where he read an antislavery paper called the *Liberator*. The messages in the paper inspired Frederick to speak out against slavery. He traveled all over the northeastern United States and talked about freedom for all. He also wrote a book called *Narrative Life of Frederick Douglass*. The book sold 5,000 copies, but Frederick realized—too late—that by putting the name of his former owner in the book, he could be found and returned to slavery.

Frederick sailed for England to be safe. He gave speeches all over Europe. Some British people paid for his freedom, so Frederick returned home to the United States. He worked for the Underground Railroad to rescue slaves, established his own newspaper, wrote books, and spoke for freedom.

During the Civil War, he organized a company of black soldiers. He asked President Lincoln to give them equal pay with other soldiers. Congress granted equal pay near the end of the Civil War.

Frederick dedicated his life to fight for justice and independence for himself and others.

YOU CAN BE A HERO	Frederick spoke up for equal rights for everyone. Are there ways you can speak up for equal rights at home? At school? In your neighborhood?

71

"BORN A SLAVE SOMEWHERE IN TENNESSEE, MARY LIVED TO BECOME ONE OF THE FREEST SOULS EVER TO DRAW BREATH, OR A .38."
— GARY COOPER

"STAGECOACH MARY" FIELDS

1832–1914

SPECIAL POWERS:	CONFIDENCE	COMPASSION

Stagecoach Mary got her name because from 1885-1893, she drove the mail from Cascade, Montana, to Saint Peter's Mission—a ten-mile journey. She was the first black woman to work for the United States Postal Service and her mail was never late. When her wagon got stuck in a snowstorm, Mary slung the mail pack over her shoulder and snowshoed the rest of the way to get there on time. She wasn't afraid of hard work.

Mary was born a slave in Hickman County, Tennessee. As a child, she loved to run and ride horses. Her best friend was Dolly Dunn, the master's daughter. When the girls grew up, Dolly left home to become a nun and changed her name to Mother Amadeus. She wanted Mary to come to her mission near Cascade, Montana.

Mary traveled to the mission where she repaired buildings, tended the garden, and helped with the animals. Mother Amadeus got pneumonia and Mary nursed her back to health.

Mary loved the rough life of Montana. She always carried a gun and could shoot straight—especially in a gunfight. But Mary was too rough for the mission, and the bishop told Mother Amadeus that Mary couldn't stay.

After that, Mary tried opening a restaurant, but she was so kind, she gave away food to anyone who was hungry whether they could pay or not. Her business ran out of money. She loved to tend the children of the town whenever they needed someone, but that didn't make her a living.

So, when the Pony Express was looking for a mail driver, Mary signed up. A lot of other men applied for the job, but Mary hitched her team up the fastest and the boss hired her. Bandits didn't rob her mail pouch because they knew she was a crack shot. She kept wolves from getting her supplies, and townspeople said she was as tough as a grizzly bear.

She retired after driving eight years and opened a laundry. Once, a man refused to pay for his clean clothes, so Mary pulled her gun and told him to pay. He did.

She loved baseball and rooted for the Cascade team when they played at home. She picked a bouquet of flowers from her garden for every player that hit a home run.

The city of Cascade loved Mary. On her birthday, the whole town closed school to celebrate. She died in 1914 and had one of the largest funerals Cascade had ever seen. Willing to work hard and make a difference, Mary had showed how to be both kind *and* tough to help the people she loved.

YOU CAN BE A HERO	Mary liked doing nice things for others. The children loved to play with her and the baseball players enjoyed her flowers. What kind of nice things can you do for others?

"I DO NOT
THINK THAT MY
LIFE IS MORE
IMPORTANT
THAN 7,000
JEWS."
—GEORG
FERDINAND
DUCKWITZ

H-1418

GEORG FERDINAND DUCKWITZ

1904–1968

SPECIAL POWERS:	COURAGE	COMPASSION	INTEGRITY

Before World War II, Georg was a coffee merchant in Germany and knew a lot of people. At first, he joined the Nazi party because he was a loyal German, but as the war broke out, he watched in horror as the Nazis devastated countries and killed Jews. Showing remarkable integrity, he courageously resigned from the party and quit his job in the Nazi Office of Foreign Affairs saying, "I am no longer able to work within this movement as an honest person."

A few years later, the government assigned him to work at the German embassy in Copenhagen, Denmark. His boss, Werner Best, informed Georg that all the Danish Jews would be sent to Theresienstadt, a German death camp on October 1, 1942.

Georg did not want his friends sent to a concentration camp. He flew to Germany to try to get the Nazis to change their orders. They refused. Then he flew to Stockholm, Sweden, to see if they would take the Danish Jews if they fled from Denmark. Sweden agreed.

Georg hurried back to Denmark and secretly told Hans Hedtoft, prime minister of Denmark, the Nazi plan. Hedtoft immediately informed Copenhagen's Jewish leaders of the plan, and the Jews began their escape. The Danish underground resistance sprang into action and hid the Jews while they waited to leave the country.

Large fishing boats were readied to travel at night across the sea that separated Denmark from Sweden. The boat trip took about an hour. Georg made sure the German patrol boats weren't around when the fishing boats left Denmark. Groups of Jews shuttled onto the boats a few at a time so the Germans wouldn't notice.

One young couple and their baby stepped into a boat. All the Jews had to climb down into the hold where the fish were kept until the boat was out to sea. The smell was awful, and the baby began to cry. The captain told the couple to get out of the boat or leave the baby in Denmark. The couple got out. Had they missed their chance to escape to freedom? They tried again the next night, and this time they gave the baby some sleeping medicine so it made no noise. They escaped to Sweden.

In three weeks, the Danish fishermen rescued 7,200 Jews and 700 family members to freedom in Sweden.

Georg's courage and compassion defied hatred and prejudice. His integrity, along with the brave actions of the many who helped him, saved almost 8,000 people from the Nazis. He is included in the Yad Vashem, Israel's official Holocaust memorial.

YOU CAN BE A HERO	Georg refused to help the Nazis when they bullied others. Instead, he tried to find ways to help those in need. What can you do to help those who are in need?

"HE WAS THE
RIGHTFUL WINNER.
HE CREATED A GAP
THAT I COULDN'T
HAVE CLOSED."
—IVÁN FERNÁNDEZ

IVÁN FERNÁNDEZ

SPECIAL POWERS:	INTEGRITY	FITNESS

ván was born in 1983 in Spain and loved to run. He became a long-distance runner and competed all over the world. But it wasn't Iván's victories that caught the world's attention—it was his integrity.

In 2013, he was just coming up to the finish line in the Burlada cross-country race in Navarre, Spain. Ahead of him was his competitor, Abel Mutai. Abel was only a few yards away from the end of the race and was about to win, but he became confused about where the finish line was. Iván could have bounded ahead and won first place, but he knew that Abel had been in front of him.

Iván showed Abel where the finish line was and guided him toward it, staying just a little behind Abel. Abel finished the race first with Iván's help and won, and Iván took second place. The video of Iván and Abel went viral and was seen throughout the world.

About the race, Iván said, "I didn't deserve to win it." He continued, "I also think that I have earned more of a name having done what I did than if I had won. And that is very important, because today, with the way things are in all circles, in soccer, in society, in politics, where it seems anything goes, a gesture of honesty goes down well."

Martín Fiz, Iván's coach, was upset with Iván and told him he should always try to win. But Iván was happy he had been honest. That was more important.

You can watch the YouTube video yourself and remember, like Iván, that kindness and fair play are more important than winning.

YOU CAN BE A HERO	Iván could have taken advantage of Abel and won the race, but he wanted to be honest and fair. Think of a way you have been honest and fair in the past week. What are some other ways you can be fair to others?

"I READ WHEN I'M DRYING MY HAIR.
I READ IN THE BATH. I READ WHEN
I'M SITTING IN THE BATHROOM.
PRETTY MUCH ANYWHERE I CAN DO
THE JOB ONE-HANDED, I READ."
–J. K. ROWLING

J. K. ROWLING

1965–

SPECIAL POWERS:	CREATIVITY	COMPASSION

J. K. Rowling is a private person, and she wanted to keep her life quiet. She might have been able to do that, until a boy named Harry Potter moved her life in a different—even magical—direction.

Joanne Rowling was born in Yate, England. Her father worked in a factory and her mother stayed home to take care of Joanne and her younger sister, Dianne. Joanne loved listening to her father read books like *The Wind in the Willows* by Kenneth Grahame. After she read the Richard Scarry books, she wrote a book about Miss Bee and her friend rabbit who was sick with the measles. She was only age six.

When she was nine, her family moved to Tutshill, a beautiful town near the Welsh border. In school, she loved reading The Chronicles of Narnia series by C.S. Lewis and *The Railway Children* by Edith Nesbit. But math was hard, and she had to practice her math facts.

In high school, her favorite subject was English, but her parents wanted her to study French and Greek. They told her she couldn't get a job if she studied English. As her parents wished, Joanne studied French and Greek while in college at Exeter, but she wasn't excited about the subjects. Still, she graduated with a degree in French and the classics.

One day, while riding on the train, Harry Potter entered her mind. She knew he would be part of a great story. Though it was a difficult time in her life, she worked hard to finish writing *Harry Potter and the Sorcerer's Stone*. The trouble was, no one wanted to publish it. They said the book was too long and talked about witchcraft. After many tries with many publishers, Bloomsbury finally published the book in 1997 but only printed 500 copies. The book sold out in four days—an instant success. Scholastic purchased the book in America and gave Joanne over $100,000.

It took her seventeen years to complete the entire seven-book series, and it went on to sell more than 400 million copies in over sixty languages. She signed books all over the world, appeared on television, sold the movie rights, and even spoke at Harvard's graduation ceremony. Her life did become public, and her fans adored her and her books.

After finishing the Harry Potter series, Joanne dove into humanitarian work. She donated to Amnesty International, multiple sclerosis research, and the National Council for One Parent Families. She also created Lumos, a charity of her own to help children grow up in loving families instead of orphanages. Joanne's life magically grew beyond the simple life she'd planned to one of changing the world for good through abundant creativity and compassion.

YOU CAN BE A HERO	Many publishers turned down Joanne's ideas for the Harry Potter books. What do you think gave her the ability to keep trying? Is there a dream you have? What will help you keep trying when others say you should give up?

"IT WAS IMPERATIVE
TO STRIKE BEFORE WE
WERE STRUCK BY THIS
OVERWHELMING FORCE
IN A HAND-TO-HAND
FIGHT. . . . I ORDERED
THE BAYONET. THE
WORD WAS ENOUGH."
—JOSHUA CHAMBERLAIN

JOSHUA CHAMBERLAIN

1828–1914

SPECIAL POWERS:	COURAGE	LEADERSHIP

Joshua Lawrence Chamberlain told his father he did not want to be a soldier, but he ended up being one of the greatest fighters in the Civil War.

As a little boy in Brewer, Maine, Joshua had a speech impediment, but by the time he graduated from Bowdoin College, he had overcome it. He went on to give many speeches and to teach college as a professor. He loved learning languages. He studied hard so he could speak English, Greek, Latin, Spanish, German, French, Italian, Arabic, French, Hebrew, and Syriac.

Joshua's father, grandfather, and great-grandfathers were all soldiers. When the Civil War began, Joshua changed his mind about not becoming a soldier and joined the 20th Maine Regiment in the Union army. At the Battle of Gettysburg, Joshua was colonel of his regiment. They were assigned to Little Round Top hill—the very end of the Union line. If Joshua's regiment didn't hold their position, the Confederate army would be able to sweep around the Union army and attack from behind. The most important battle of the war could be lost.

Sure enough, the Confederate soldiers attacked the hill. They started to push the Union back. The Confederates repeatedly fired on the 20th Maine Regiment. It looked like the Confederates would take the hill. Joshua didn't want that to happen. When his regiment started running low on ammunition, he waved his bayonet and shouted for a charge. His bravery inspired his soldiers, and they ran forward through the woods at the Confederate soldiers. A bullet hit Joshua's sword scabbard, bruising his hip, and another hit his right foot, but he kept going. He captured a Confederate soldier and held his bayonet at the man's throat. Another Confederate officer shot at Joshua, barely missing his head. Joshua captured that officer, too, and seized his gun. Joshua's regiment protected Little Round Top and held their position, saving the Union army from a disastrous defeat. Joshua received a Medal of Honor for his bravery.

Years later, on April 9, 1865, General Lee, head of the Confederate army, assigned General Gordon to surrender to the Union. Joshua, now a general himself, was the officer who accepted the surrender of arms and colors. As the defeated Confederate soldiers marched by, Joshua signaled his soldiers to "carry arms" (rifle held in the right hand, barrel against the shoulder) as a sign of respect for their Confederate brothers. General Gordon wheeled his horse around and pointed his sword to his stirrup, indicating for the Confederate soldiers to dip their colors and respond to the carry. Both armies showed respect for each other because of Joshua's leadership.

Joshua fought in twenty Civil War battles and had six horses shot from under him. He was wounded six times and received honors for bravery four times. He went home to become President of Bowdoin College and later served four terms as Governor of Maine. But Joshua, the man who never wanted to fight, is remembered mostly for his bravery at the Battle of Gettysburg in the Civil War. His courage and leadership saved the battle, and that battle saved the country.

YOU CAN BE A HERO	Joshua didn't want to fight, but when he did, he did so brilliantly and with honor because he knew it was right. What is something you know is right to do? Think of how you could do it with your whole heart.

"PEOPLE WHO LOVE TO EAT ARE THE BEST PEOPLE."
—JULIA CHILD

JULIA CHILD

1912–2004

SPECIAL POWERS:	CREATIVITY	HUMOR

Julia loved to eat. While taping a television show, she held a spatula covered with chocolate cake batter up to the camera and said, "We have this little bit on the edge of the spatula which is for the cook. It's part of the recipe!" Another time, while flipping a potato cake, she tossed it into the air and it fell apart—some landed in the pan and some all over the stove. She scooped up as much of it as she could and put it back in the pan. "You're alone in the kitchen—who is going to see?" she told the camera and went on to say that to get better, you must practice. She was so funny and creative that everyone loved her show.

Julia Carolyn McWilliams grew up in Pasadena, California. She was tall and enjoyed sports. She joined the drama club. For high school, she attended a boarding school and then went on to Smith College in Massachusetts. After graduating, she got a job writing press releases, but she was bored. When World War II broke out, she got a position with the present-day Central Intelligence Agency (CIA) and was sent to India. There she met Paul Child. The two became good friends.

Paul was soon transferred to China and Julia followed. Julia had lived in the United States all her life and hadn't experienced the world like Paul had. He introduced her to good Chinese food, and Julia loved it. After the war, they decided to get married. Paul, who worked for the State Department, was transferred to Paris, France. There, Julia fell in love with French cooking.

She decided to enroll in Le Cordon Bleu cooking school. The head of the school placed her in a beginner's class because she was a woman—and an American. The headmistress didn't like Americans. But Julia wanted to be in the professional's class with the men. She argued until she got her way.

While in Paris, she became friends with Simca Beck. Along with another friend, they decided to write a French cookbook for American women. They called the book *Mastering the Art of French Cooking*. Many didn't believe Americans would want the book, but Julia was right. The cookbook was a runaway hit.

In 1961, the Boston television station WGBH signed Julia up for a cooking show. She was an instant success because of her natural, genuine style. She was a television star for the next forty years. She had a great sense of humor, and she helped her viewers believe they could become good cooks.

Julia went on to publish lots of cookbooks and do many more television series. In 2003, she received the US Presidential Medal of Freedom. She donated her kitchen to the Smithsonian Institution's museum for everyone to see.

Julia's creative cooking style and good humor gave people the courage to try new things and love life the way she did. To her, life was a delicious meal to savor. Family, friends, food, and laughter offer rich possibilities each day. So dig in! Or, as she would probably put it herself, "Bon appétit!"

YOU CAN BE A HERO	Julia loved life and cooking and making friends. What do you love to do? How can you enjoy the things you love and make friends along the way?

"I NEVER TOOK ANY
CREDIT BECAUSE WE
ALWAYS WORKED AS A
TEAM; IT WAS NEVER
JUST ONE PERSON."
– KATHERINE JOHNSON

KATHERINE JOHNSON

1918–

SPECIAL POWERS:	INTELLIGENCE	PERSEVERANCE

Katherine loved to count. She counted the steps from her house to the church. She counted the dishes and silverware when she cleaned up after dinner. She loved numbers.

She was born in White Sulphur Springs, West Virginia. When her older brothers and sisters went to school, she didn't want to be left behind. She was very smart, and at age five she started second grade. By the time she was ten, she enrolled in high school.

Her family split their time between their home in White Sulphur Springs and West Virginia State University in Charleston, where there was a high school that African Americans could attend. Katherine graduated from the high school at age fourteen.

Katherine stayed on at West Virginia State University for college. She was very good at math, but she also loved French. Her professors told her she could pick only one major, but she found a way to complete classes in both math *and* French. She earned two bachelor's degrees by the time she was eighteen, graduating with honors.

The government's space program, NASA, was hiring mathematicians, and Katherine got a job doing the calculations for the astronaut's space ships. The women who worked there were called "human computers" because they did the job computers do today. The engineers could tell that Katherine was very intelligent because she asked a lot of questions about how things worked. The engineers began to include her in their meetings because they trusted her to make sure the space ship was going in the right direction—whether it was to the moon or back home.

When Alan Shepard went into space in 1961, Katherine made the calculations for his flight path and landing back to earth. By the next year, NASA had installed machine computers to figure the direction of the space ship. But John Glenn, who was the first astronaut to orbit the earth, didn't trust the new machines. He asked Katherine to manually check the computer's math. She did and found it to be correct.

Katherine and her team also worked to put the astronauts on the moon. When Neil Armstrong, Buzz Aldrin Jr., and Michael Collins flew to the moon, Katherine was their backup. She and her team made sure that if anything went wrong, there was a plan to keep them safe.

In 2015, she was awarded the Presidential Medal of Freedom by President Obama, and in 2016, NASA named a research facility in her honor: The Katherine G. Johnson Computational Research Facility.

Certainly, Katherine's intelligence and perseverance broke down the barriers to space. But more importantly, she showed everyone how to break down barriers to equality, and that might have been her greatest computation of all.

YOU CAN BE A HERO	Katherine lived at a time when many people were biased against women and African Americans. She worked hard to show them what she could do. Do people ever doubt your abilities? What could you do? And what could you do to help others believe in themselves?

"I JUST WANT TO GET BETTER AT THE THINGS I DON'T KNOW. THAT'S THE GOAL."
—LIN-MANUEL MIRANDA

LIN-MANUEL MIRANDA

1980 –

SPECIAL POWERS:	CREATIVITY	HARD WORK

Lin-Manuel felt like an outsider. His parents were Puerto Rican, so he was different from the white kids that attended with him at Hunter College Elementary for gifted students. Since his school was in the Upper East Side of New York City, he didn't play much with the kids in his neighborhood. He spent the summers with his grandparents in Puerto Rico, and the kids there called him a *gringo* because he lived in the United States.

His father said that at his first elementary school piano recital, his eyes lit up when people clapped for him, so he played another song and still another. The people clapped each time. Finally, the teacher told Lin-Manuel that the other children needed a turn to play.

As a child, Lin-Manuel loved to listen to music. He memorized the lyrics of several Broadway musicals. He loved Disney musicals—especially *The Little Mermaid*. He was fascinated by Sebastian, who performed the calypso number underwater. He loved all kinds of music—especially rap.

After school, he shouldered his videotape camcorder and asked the neighborhood kids if they wanted to make movies. They all did. During the summers in Puerto Rico, his grandfather brought the surveillance camera home from his job at the credit union so Lin-Manuel could film his stories. He also wrote and performed in several musicals in high school.

In college, he wrote a musical called *In the Heights*. Everyone enjoyed it. Other professionals helped Lin-Manuel make it even better. The musical made it to Off-Broadway (shows start here and are reworked until they are good enough for Broadway). After a little more refining, *In the Heights* was ready for Broadway itself, and Lin-Manuel had finally made it. The show ran from 2007–2011 and won Tony Awards and Grammy Awards.

While on vacation, Lin-Manuel read the book *Hamilton* and decided to do a musical about the life of Alexander Hamilton, one of the Founding Fathers of the United States. He wrote over the next six years, consulted with the author of the book and other musical theater experts, and finally finished *Hamilton: An American Musical* in 2015. Lin-Manuel wrote the play, the songs, and took the lead role. The musical played Off-Broadway for just a few months and then hit Broadway with a smash. Tickets sold out for over a year in advance!

Lin-Manuel also worked with Disney on the music for *Moana*, *Star Wars: The Force Awakens*, *Duck Tales*, and *Mary Poppins Returns*, where he also played the lamplighter, Jack.

For his work, Lin-Manuel won a Pulitzer Prize, three Tony Awards, three Grammys, and an Emmy, and was nominated for an Academy Award. Though he might have felt like an outsider as a child, creativity and hard work lifted him above it to fill the world with the light and magic of powerful music.

YOU CAN BE A HERO	Lin-Manuel loved music, but he had to practice and work hard to make musicals people would enjoy. What do you love to do? Are you working hard and practicing so you can share your talent with others?

"MUSIC COMES TO
ME MORE READILY
THAN WORDS."
—LUDWIG VAN
BEETHOVEN

LUDWIG VAN BEETHOVEN

1770–1827

SPECIAL POWERS:	CREATIVITY	PERSEVERANCE

Ludwig grew up surrounded by music, but his childhood wasn't easy. His father and his grandfather were both court musicians. His first teacher was his father who made him practice all day. He could be very strict. Sometimes, he dragged Ludwig out of bed in the middle of the night and sat him at the piano. Ludwig cried, but that only made his father angry—he wanted him to be another Mozart. But Ludwig didn't want to play the music like his father told him. He wanted to play music his own way.

Ludwig played his first concert when he was seven. (His father said he was six.) The court decided he needed a new teacher. Christian Gottlob Neefe, who was the court organist, taught Ludwig to play the organ and how to compose music. Ludwig was glad to have a kind teacher.

When he was sixteen, he went to Vienna, Austria. He intended to study with Mozart, but his mother became ill, so Ludwig returned home immediately. She died shortly thereafter. His father became very ill too, so Ludwig had to raise his two younger brothers.

Ludwig supported them the best he could. He played the viola in the court orchestra. He met the famous composer, Joseph Haydn, and studied with him for a while.

He moved to Vienna and published several piano concertos and other pieces. Many people thought his melodies were so beautiful, they cried.

He continued to compose and play for the nobility, but he was becoming deaf. Soon he couldn't perform like he used to. He left Vienna to live in the country. He took long walks in the woods. He especially loved the crashing of lightning and the rumble of thunderstorms. In his Fifth Symphony, you can hear the booming thunder.

Ludwig still wanted to conduct the orchestra, but because of his deafness, the musicians got mixed up and couldn't follow him. When he composed his Ninth Symphony, he said he would watch the musicians very carefully so he could lead the orchestra and chorus one last time. He conducted the first performance of the symphony in Vienna. Everyone loved it. People stood and clapped and cheered. But Ludwig didn't know it. One of the singers stood up on the podium and turned him around so he could see the audience. He was so happy that he cried.

Today, Ludwig is still one of the most famous composers in the world. His music is known for its passion and tenderness—things that Ludwig's challenges helped him feel deeply. With perseverance and creativity, he had turned hardship into beauty—music the whole world would enjoy for centuries to come.

YOU CAN BE A HERO	Ludwig had some hard things happen to him in his life. But he didn't quit. He kept going and became the best he could be. Do you have challenges in your life? What are your hard things? Will you let them stop you or will you keep going? What will you do to become the best you can be?

"I USED TO BE VERY
SHY AND AVOID
ALL COMPANY. . . . I
COULD NOT BEAR TO
TALK TO ANYBODY."
—MOHANDAS GANDHI

MOHANDAS GANDHI

1841–1898

SPECIAL POWERS:	LEADERSHIP	INDEPENDENCE	SACRIFICE

Gandhi grew up in India when the British ruled his country. He was born in Porbandar on India's western coast on the Arabic Sea. He was a shy child, having a difficulty with communication that followed him into his teenage years. A family friend wanted Gandhi to go into politics, so his parents sent him to school in England to become a lawyer. But when he took his first case, he was so shy that he couldn't speak in court, forcing his clients to find another attorney.

There was a job opening in South Africa, so Gandhi sailed there. After he landed, he took the train to get to his work. He paid for a comfortable first-class compartment. When a European man told him to get out of the train car because he had dark skin, Gandhi didn't move. He had paid for a first-class ticket, and he wanted to sit first class. Because Gandhi wouldn't leave, the conductor threw him off the train.

Gandhi was upset and decided he had to find the courage to speak up for the rights of his people. While he was in Africa, he asked the government to treat the people from India with respect, but they didn't listen. Gandhi organized the Indians to quit work until an unfair tax was abolished. Because all the Indians stayed home from their jobs, the government listened. Gandhi won peaceful change with his gentle but powerful ways.

Gandhi returned to India to work for freedom for his people. Indians heard about what he did in South Africa and called him "Mahatma," meaning "The Great Soul." Gandhi wanted the British to treat Indians fairly, but they didn't. He tried talking with the British rulers, but they wouldn't listen. The Indians were charged tax for their salt, so Gandhi led a peaceful march to the sea for everyone to get their own salt. The British began to listen.

The Indians were mostly split into two religious groups: Hindus and Muslims. They often didn't like each other and got into fights. Gandhi told them that peace was the only way. He wouldn't eat until the people quit fighting. Everyone worried he would die, so they began to be more tolerant of each other.

Gandhi stood up for India's rights and independence—for both Hindus and Muslims. In doing so, he sacrificed food, comfort, and eventually, his very own life. His leadership won peaceful change for his people. He freed the entire country from unfair rule with his gentle ways.

YOU CAN BE A HERO	Gandhi was shy when he was young, but he learned to talk about problems and discuss ways to solve them. What can you do to help those around you have a better life? Can you talk about problems and suggest ways to solve them?

"PEACE BEGINS
WITH A SMILE."
–MOTHER TERESA

MOTHER TERESA

1910–1997

SPECIAL POWERS:	COMPASSION	SACRIFICE

Anjezë Gonxhe Bojaxhiu grew up in a happy family in Skopje, Macedonia. When she was young, she became very interested in missionaries who traveled to different lands to teach and help the poor. She studied about missionaries in India. As soon as she was eighteen, she joined the Catholic nuns who worked in Calcutta, India, and changed her name to Mary Teresa.

Mary Teresa spoke five languages, but the most important ones would be Bengali and Hindi because she would use those to help the people she served in India. At first, she taught geography and history at a girl's school called Loreto Convent Entally. But when she saw all the poor people afflicted with disease and poverty outside the school walls, she knew those were the people she wanted to help.

Mary got permission from the Mother General and Pope Pius XII to serve the poor of India. She first went to the Holy Family Hospital to work with the nurses and doctors so she could learn about surgery and medicine.

In 1948, she put on a white sari with a blue border and went into the slums of Moti Jheel. Under the direction of the Pope, she organized the Missionaries of Charity. "Never let anyone come to you without coming away better and happier," she told the sisters.

Next, she asked the government for a place where the dying could be comforted. They gave her an abandoned Hindi temple. She continued working, and soon, Mary had so many sisters in her Missionaries of Charity that she needed a bigger house. They named it Mother House and began calling her Mother Teresa. She then founded another home, Shishu Bhavan, as a place for expectant mothers, abandoned children, the handicapped, and the sick to stay. The home also included a soup kitchen.

The government also gave Mother Teresa land to begin a leper colony where the lepers built their own houses and grew their own food. She established schools for children of all ages that taught not only reading and writing, but also carpentry and childcare. The Church also approved her founding the Missionary Brothers of Charity.

People all over the world heard of Mother Teresa's work, and money poured in to help her. She organized a Missionaries of Charity Foundation and missions were established all over the world. Today, there are over 400,000 who work for her cause to help the poor.

Mother Teresa received many awards, including the Nobel Peace Prize. When she died, her body was drawn through the streets of Calcutta on the same carriage that had held Mahatma Gandhi's during his funeral. In 2016, the Catholic Church gave her the high honor of becoming a Saint.

Mother Teresa dedicated her life to lifting up those who had been forgotten by almost everyone else. She was quiet and soft, yet her wordless sermons on kindness and charity reached the hearts of the entire world. The world can be a noisy, turbulent place, but she showed that compassion can be the strongest voice of all.

YOU CAN BE A HERO	Mother Teresa showed gentle compassion. What do those words means to you? How can you be gentle and kind to others?

"TRUTH AND
CLARITY ARE
COMPLEMENTARY."
—NIELS BOHR

NIELS BOHR

1885–1962

SPECIAL POWERS:	INTELLIGENCE	COMPASSION

As a child, Niels always had to get the details just right. When his grade school teacher asked him to draw a specific house, he counted the pickets in the fence before he began to draw to make sure he was accurate. He was a good student and loved to read. But his passions were math and physics, and when he grew up, he became a brilliant research scientist.

After he graduated from college in Denmark, he went to England to study the quantum theory of atoms and how electron particles worked. He became friends with his professor, Ernest Rutherford. Niels's research led to imaging devices used in hospitals today, like CAT scans and MRI machines. Niels also became friends with Albert Einstein. They disagreed sometimes, but they enjoyed debating with each other.

Niels wanted to build a physics institute in Copenhagen, Denmark, so he raised much of the money himself. Because he was such a good researcher, many students from around the world studied with him. He received a Nobel Prize in 1922.

During World War II, when the Germans occupied Denmark, the British sent Niels a secret key with tiny microfilm inside. On the film was a message urging him to escape to England. But Niels loved Denmark, where he was born, and he refused to leave. Instead, he invited many Jewish-German scientists to his physics institute to escape from Hitler. Niels was friends with scientists all over the world, and he found jobs for many of them. Then in 1943, Niels learned that the Germans planned to capture all the Jews in Denmark and send them to concentration camps. He knew that he and his family had to get away because Niels's mother was Jewish. They escaped to Sweden on a fishing boat.

Niels's family remained in Sweden while he flew to England in a plane called a Mosquito. The fast plane flew at high altitudes to avoid enemy fighters, but the plane was not pressurized and Niels was in the back with no oxygen. He passed out. When they landed, he regained consciousness and was all right.

He later flew to Los Alamos, New Mexico, where scientists were developing the atom bomb. He helped design the device that would start the chain reaction of one of the bombs.

But Niels worried about the devastation the bomb could cause. He wanted atomic energy used for good things, not war. He met with both President Roosevelt and Winston Churchill and asked them to seek peace. He sent a letter to the United Nations, asking for international talks. For his work, he received the Atoms for Peace award in 1957.

Knowledge can be a challenging thing. Over the centuries, it has often been used for good—and for bad. And sometimes, the difference between what's good and what's bad can seem confusing indeed. Today, the world still debates whether the atomic bomb should have been created. But one thing is for certain: Niels was a compassionate man who tried to use his intelligence for the benefit of all. And if the world can follow that example, perhaps there wouldn't be a need for bombs at all.

YOU CAN BE A HERO	Niels wanted his discoveries used for good things, not bad. Many of them are used for good today. How can you use the things you learn for good?

"I AM NATURALLY FOND
OF ADVENTURE, A LITTLE
AMBITIOUS, AND A GOOD
DEAL ROMANTIC—BUT
PATRIOTISM WAS THE TRUE
SECRET OF MY SUCCESS."
—SARAH EMMA EDMONDS

SARAH EMMA EDMONDS

1841–1898

SPECIAL POWERS:	COURAGE	CONFIDENCE

When she was sixteen, Emma Edmonds, as she liked to be called, came to the United States from Canada looking for adventure.

When the Civil War broke out in 1861, Emma wanted to fight. So, she joined the Union army—as a man. She cut her brown wavy hair and dressed in pants, then marched into the recruiting office in Flint, Michigan, and enlisted as Franklin Thompson. She gave her occupations as Bible salesman and medical orderly. The officer signed her up and sent Franklin directly to the supply tent for her uniform. Emma was now "Private Thompson" of the Second Michigan Volunteers, US Army.

"Private Thompson" was assigned to the medical unit with Dr. Hodes and went immediately to Washington, DC, where she nursed injured soldiers. After several months, the Second Michigan Volunteers transferred to Fort Monroe, Virginia, under the direction of General George McClellan.

The Union army needed spies to find out the Confederate army's plans. Emma decided this was her chance. She had enjoyed working as a nurse, but she wanted more excitement. Still pretending to be Private Thompson, she told General McClellan's officers that she wanted to be a spy. The staff peppered her with questions about weapons and the Union's cause and even gave her a phrenology test (felt the bumps on her head) to see if she was brave and secretive. She passed all the tests and became a spy.

For her first assignment, she got a black, wooly wig, darkened her skin with silver nitrate, and pretended to be a black man named Cuff. Behind enemy lines, she hauled wheelbarrows full of gravel with other slaves and learned enemy plans and positions. The Confederate officer in charge gave her a rifle and assigned her guard duty that night. When everyone was asleep, she took her new rifle and slipped back behind the Union lines to report to McClellan.

On another mission, she dressed as Bridget O'Shea, an old Irish peddler. She found a young Confederate soldier, dying of typhoid fever. The soldier handed her a gold watch to take to his commanding officer after he died. This gave "Bridget" an excuse to visit the Confederate officer's quarters to gather more information. She was given a horse to help recover the young soldier's body. Afterwards, the officer assigned her a lookout post, and she escaped behind Union lines with the horse.

Emma served many spy missions that helped the Union army to victory. After the war, a group of Civil War veterans called the Grand Army of the Republic recognized Emma for her service. She was the only female member they ever honored.

When the war ended, Emma traveled back to Canada and married an old friend. They returned to Ohio and had three sons—one joined the US Army like his mother. Her courage had inspired her family, her country, and the generations who followed to believe that they, too, could make a difference.

YOU CAN BE A HERO	Emma loved adventure. She wasn't afraid to try new things. Name one new thing you did in the past week. Would you do it again? Did it make you feel adventurous?

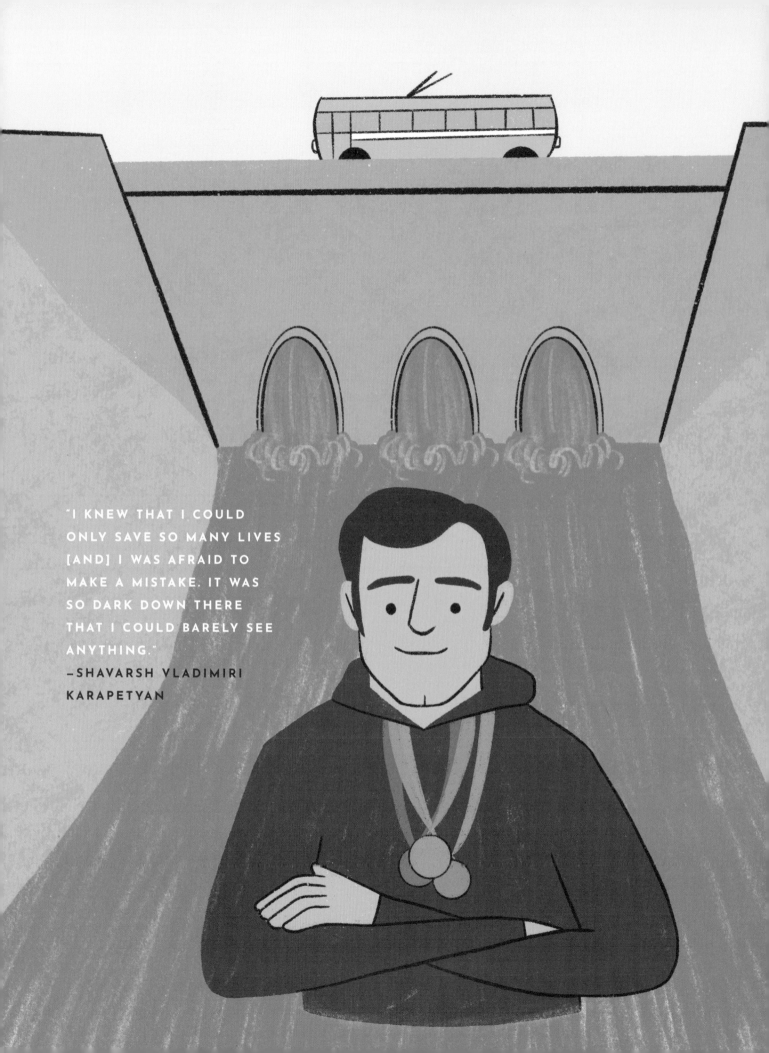

"I KNEW THAT I COULD ONLY SAVE SO MANY LIVES [AND] I WAS AFRAID TO MAKE A MISTAKE. IT WAS SO DARK DOWN THERE THAT I COULD BARELY SEE ANYTHING."
—SHAVARSH VLADIMIRI KARAPETYAN

SHAVARSH VLADIMIRI KARAPETYAN

1953–

SPECIAL POWERS:	FITNESS	SACRIFICE

Shavarsh was born in Armenia, then part of the Soviet Union, in 1953. From an early age, he loved to swim. As he grew older, he decided that finswimming was his favorite sport. In finswimming, fins and a snorkel are used, and one's face must be immersed in the water at all times. Shavarsh was good at it. He became a master swimmer and broke the world record at international competitions ten times! But more incredible still was how Shavarsh sacrificed that promising sports career to help others in need.

One afternoon in 1976, he and his brother were running along the edge of Yerevan Lake when they saw a trolleybus careen out of control and crash off the edge of a dam. Shavarsh dove into the icy waters immediately. As the bus sank, silt and sewage from the bottom billowed up around him so that he could hardly see.

The bus was crowded with ninety-two people trapped inside. He had to get them out. Thinking fast, he knocked the back windows out with his legs. Glass shards cut him and filthy water got into his lungs, but he kept working. He knew he couldn't save them all, but he wanted to get as many out as he could and worked quickly. His lungs were strong because of his competitive swimming. He dragged people out one-by-one and saved twenty before he passed out from the icy water, the glass cuts all over his body, and the sewer water he had swallowed. At the hospital, he lay in a coma for forty-five days. His body was infected with sepsis because of the raw sewage. He recovered, but because of the damage to his body, he would never be able to compete in finswimming again.

Pictures of the accident were kept in the district attorney's office and no one saw them for two years. Then *Pravda*, the Soviet Union's newspaper, published an article entitled "The Underwater Battle of the Champion." He became famous overnight and received 60,000 letters.

But Shavarsh's heroic actions didn't stop there. Several years later, in 1985, he saw a burning building. He ran inside and saved those caught in the fire. He was severely burned and was again hospitalized, but he recovered.

He moved to Moscow and opened a shoe company called Second Breath. He received the UNESCO Fair Play award and an asteroid was named after him. In the 2014 Winter Olympics in Russia, he carried the torch twice through Moscow.

Shavarsh will be remembered as a talented athlete who courageously sacrificed his gift so that others could live. He reminded the world that whatever gifts one might have, those gifts are best used in the serving and uplifting of others.

YOU CAN BE A HERO	Shavarsh sacrificed his swimming career to save the lives of twenty people. You may not be asked to save lives, but there are ways you can help others. What have you done to make a difference in someone's life today?

"ON MY UNDERGROUND RAILROAD I
NEBBER RUN MY TRAIN OFF DE TRACK
AND I NEBBER LOS' A PASSENGER."
–HARRIET TUBMAN

HARRIET TUBMAN

1820–1913

SPECIAL POWERS:	COURAGE	LEADERSHIP

arriet grew up in slavery. She always felt uneasy whenever a white man came around because two of her sisters had been sold to slave owners further south. Harriet never knew if she would be next. From the time she was five, she was hired out to work for other people, and her master kept all the money she earned. She cleaned houses during the day and rocked babies at night. She wasn't considered a person—just a slave—so no one thought she needed to sleep, even though she was a small child.

One day, while working the field, she saw a slave named Jim running away. The master threw a brick at Jim, but the brick hit Harriet instead, almost killing her. Her mother nursed her, and it took a long time for Harriet to recover. The blow to her head caused narcolepsy (sleep seizures), and afterwards she would fall asleep several times a day for no reason. Her master couldn't sell her because no one wanted a slave who fell asleep.

As Harriet got older, she dreamed of freedom. Her father told her that if she were to escape and avoid getting caught, she should follow the North Star, travel at night, and always wade through a river when she came to one because then the tracking dogs couldn't follow her scent.

She wanted her husband, John Tubman, to run away with her, but he wouldn't do it. So, in 1849, she ran away by herself to Philadelphia. She was lonely and wanted her family to be with her. When she went back to get John, she found he had married someone else. Her feelings were hurt so she helped other family members to freedom instead.

Harriett began to work for the Underground Railroad. She guided others to freedom, including her parents and many of her family. In all, she led over 300 slaves north, and everyone she helped made it to freedom. When one man got scared and wanted to go back, Harriet leveled at gun at him and told him she'd shoot him before she'd let him go back. She didn't want him to give away the Underground Railroad's secret hiding places. She conducted many of the slaves up to Canada where it was safe.

During the Civil War, she volunteered as a nurse, cook, scout, and even spy for the Union Army. In 1863, she led a raid up the Combahee River in South Carolina and freed 700 slaves. Her people called her Moses because she led so many to freedom. Harriett's courage was a bright light to people in times of darkness—just like the North Star she had followed so many years ago.

YOU CAN BE A HERO	Harriet had courage to stand up for freedom. She helped her family and many others find freedom so they could live their lives the way they wanted to. Make a list of the freedoms you have and try to be grateful for them each day.

"I HAVE DONE IT. . . .
NOT A LIFE WAS LOST."
—SIR EARNEST
SHACKLETON

SIR EARNEST SHACKLETON

1874–1922

SPECIAL POWERS:	LEADERSHIP	COURAGE	CONFIDENCE

Shackleton wanted adventure in his life, so he left London at age sixteen and sailed the world on merchant ships. His favorite place was Antarctica.

In 1914, Shackleton commanded the ship *Endurance* on an expedition to sail to Antarctica and cross the continent on foot. He anchored briefly on South Georgia Island at the whaling station, and then he and his men sailed on towards the continent. They saw lots of humpback and killer whales. Little penguins bowed to the ship as it passed.

Near the end of January 1915, they had picked their way through 1,000 miles of icepack, but they were still 100 miles from land. The ship was now surrounded by ice and couldn't move. They were trapped.

Shackleton was a gifted leader. To help his men not worry, he created things for them to do. He made poker chips out of whalebones and the men played cards. They held soccer games and made igloos for their dogs. They created plays, made up pantomimes, and even learned a Maori dance. When the men fought, Shackleton warned them that they had to get along if they were going to survive.

But eventually, ice pressed against the ship, crushing it into tiny pieces. Shackleton loaded the ship's supplies on sleds for the dogs to pull. He then organized the men to haul the two lifeboats over the cracked and bumpy ice to find the ocean.

They weathered storms from November 1915 through March 1916. Then, the ice began to break up. A giant iceberg plowed through the ice toward them, but they escaped.

The ice continued to melt, and finally, on April 9, 1916, they launched the lifeboats into the ocean. Gales of freezing wind lashed the men, chilling them to the bone. They wondered if they would survive. On April 15, they dragged themselves onto tiny Elephant Island—drenched, cold, and exhausted. They beached the boats, used them for shelter, and slept on the rocks.

Shackleton had to get his men home safely, and he knew no one would find them on this tiny island 581 miles from the South Georgia Island where they began their journey. No one even knew they were alive.

Shackleton and five others took one of the lifeboats to go for help. They landed on South Georgia Island and trekked over rugged mountains to get to the whaling station. Finally, after days, they reached civilization, and Shackleton immediately took boats to rescue his men back on Elephant Island.

Because of Shackleton's confident leadership and courage, he and his men made it safely home to England after being stranded for two years on the frozen Antarctic ice. Against all odds, not a single life had been lost.

YOU CAN BE A HERO	Shackleton kept his men safe, even though they were trapped by freezing weather and ice. He interested them in games and exercise. What do you do to keep life fun and get the exercise you need? Think of ways you could keep from getting bored if you were trapped by ice.

"THE ONLY
PERSON YOU
SHOULD TRY TO
BE BETTER THAN
IS THE PERSON
YOU WERE
YESTERDAY."
—GAIL HALVERSON

GAIL HALVERSON

1920–

SPECIAL POWERS:	COMPASSION	FRIENDSHIP

Gail wanted to fly airplanes from the time he was little. Even though he grew up in rural Idaho and Utah—far away from a busy airport—he loved airplanes. When he was older, he joined the Civil Air Patrol and then became a pilot for the United States Air Force during World War II.

After the war, he was assigned to fly C-47s and C-54s during the Berlin Airlift. The German people in the Russian sector of Berlin were starving, so the US military dropped food from airplanes to help them survive. Operation Vittles, as the airlift was called, saved many German lives.

On his day off, Gail wanted to see more of Berlin, so he toured the city. When he got to the Tempelhof Airport, he saw thirty children looking through the fence. Gail talked to them and took their pictures. When he was ready to leave, they wanted him to give them something. All he had were two sticks of gum—for thirty of them. They didn't grab it or try to take it away from each other. Instead, they shared tiny pieces of it all around. When the gum was gone, the children who didn't get any smelled the wrapper.

Gail told them he would drop some gum and candy for all of them out of his plane the next day. They asked how they would know it was his plane. He said he would wiggle the wings.

He and his copilot and engineer pooled their ration cards and bought as much candy as they could. The next day, Gail flew over the children, wiggled his plane's wings, and dropped the candy tied onto parachutes made from handkerchiefs. The children cheered.

Gail became known as "The Candy Bomber" and "Uncle Wiggly Wings." Other pilots decided to help, and soon, there were lots of pilots dropping candy for the children. The kids in the United States heard about it and began to donate even more candy. In all, about twenty-three tons of candy were airdropped from 250,000 parachutes in Operation Little Vittles over Berlin.

Gail stayed in the Air Force and got his master's degree in aeronautical engineering. He worked on satellite launches and orbit operations for the space program. But he also continued "The Candy Bomber" tradition by encouraging the government to drop candy in war-torn Bosnia, Japan, Guam, Albania, and Iraq. Military planes even dropped toys, teddy bears, and soccer balls for Iraqi children.

Gail has received many awards, including the Congressional Gold Medal, the National Defense Service Medal, and a bronze service star.

There are many powers in this world. Some patrol the seas in navies, some traverse the continents in armies, but some fall from the sky on tiny parachutes. Gail's compassion was a special kind of power—the kind that gives hope to children when hope seems to be lost.

YOU CAN BE A HERO	Gail gave the children in Berlin hope when they had none. The candy he dropped from tiny parachutes sent a message to them that someone cared. What can you do to show those around you that you care?

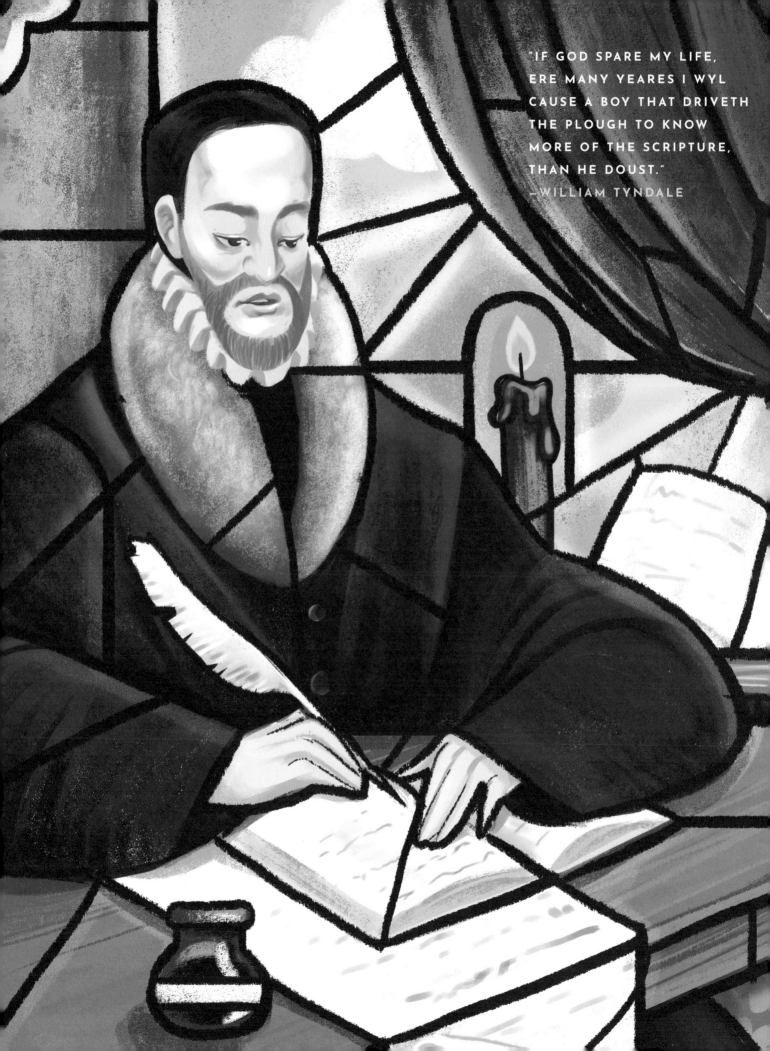

"IF GOD SPARE MY LIFE,
ERE MANY YEARES I WYL
CAUSE A BOY THAT DRIVETH
THE PLOUGH TO KNOW
MORE OF THE SCRIPTURE,
THAN HE DOUST."
—WILLIAM TYNDALE

WILLIAM TYNDALE

1494–1536

SPECIAL POWERS:	COURAGE	EDUCATION	SACRIFICE

William grew up in rural England in the Cotswolds, a farming area where sheep grazed. Merchants from all over the world came to buy fabric made from the sheep's wool. As a boy, William watched these merchants and learned about other languages and faraway lands.

William studied hard in school, and by the time he was twelve, he could speak Latin. He went on to school in Oxford and Cambridge for religious studies. There, he learned French, Hebrew, Italian, German, Spanish, and Greek—the language of the original New Testament.

William studied the New Testament in Greek. He loved reading the scriptures for himself and wanted everyone to be able to do the same. He decided to translate them into English. But in England, it was against the law to translate any part of the Bible for the common people to read.

In Germany in 1517, the same year William went to Cambridge, Martin Luther wrote a paper of ninety-five complaints against the Church. William read them and agreed with many of the things Martin Luther said. Both thought that the Church's rules should agree with the writings in the original Greek New Testament.

The Church didn't like William's new ideas, and government officials scolded him for speaking out. When he asked the Church leaders in London to help him translate the Bible into English, they turned him away. They wanted to arrest him, so he left England and went to Germany. There he found a wealthy man who agreed to support him while he worked on the translation.

Eventually, William finished translating the New Testament into English, but he needed to get it printed. The authorities found out about the first printing and hurried to stop the press. William kept the next printing a secret, and the finished books were shipped to England where people finally had a copy of the scriptures in their own language. The people loved William's beautiful writing.

Church leaders in England were angry. They burned as many copies of the English New Testament as they could find. The authorities hunted for William all over England and in other countries. They finally found him in Belgium and arrested him. In 1536, William was bound to a stake and burned to death.

But, even though he had died, William's writings spread throughout the world. His words made their way into Shakespeare's plays. They were carried aboard the Mayflower by pilgrims seeking religious freedom. They guided Abraham Lincoln's struggle to heal a divided nation. William's courage to defy oppression cost him his life, but his sacrifice unlocked words of hope and inspiration for generations to come.

YOU CAN BE A HERO	William wanted everyone to be able to read the Bible in their own language. He was thoughtful of people he didn't even know. Are there ways you can be thoughtful of others?

"[MY FATHER] SAID HE
WAS SORRY THAT HE WAS
CLOSE TO DESTROYING
MY CAREER. I TOLD HIM
I WAS LUCKY THAT I HAD
A STRONG MIND AND I
DIDN'T LISTEN TO HIM."
—TEGLA LOROUPE

TEGLA LOROUPE

1973 –

SPECIAL POWERS:	FITNESS	CONFIDENCE

When Tegla started school at age six, her elementary school was over six miles from her home. She ran barefoot to school every day. After school, she tended the cattle and worked in the fields. Her family belonged to the Pokot tribe in the northwest region of Kenya, and she had twenty-four brothers and sisters.

At school, she ran long-distance races with the older children, winning many of them. She decided to become a runner. But the athletic program said she was too small, and her father told her she should stay home to cook and care for the children.

Tegla didn't give up. Her mother believed Tegla could be whatever she wanted to be, so Tegla held fast to her dream of becoming a runner. In 1988, she won a cross-country race—barefoot. She earned enough money to buy a pair of running shoes, but she only wore them for especially rough races.

She began to compete internationally, winning the Goodwill Games in 1994 and 1998—barefoot, of course. She won the New York Marathon in 1994 and again in 1995. Girls in Africa loved her—they had a woman athlete they could be proud of. She won marathons in London (2000), Rome (2000), Lausanne (2002), Cologne (2003), Leipzig (2004), and Hong Kong (2006).

But even more than running, Tegla wanted to help the community she grew up in. The local tribes in northwest Kenya fought with each other and stole each other's cattle. She wanted her people to live in peace. In 2003, Tegla decided to establish peace marathons for the warriors of the tribes in Kenya, Uganda, and Sudan. She invited civil leaders to participate also. As a result, a lot of the warriors quit fighting.

The Kenyan government praised her for her peace efforts. She also built a school and an orphanage in Kapenguria, Kenya.

She was named United Nations Ambassador of Sport along with athletes from Switzerland, Chile, and Australia. The International Association of Athletics Federation and UNICEF also named her an International Sports Ambassador.

Tegla never gave up on her dream to run. With hard work, she rose from humble beginnings to become an international champion. But more than that, she used her fame to bring peace to her people. Tegla knew the way of a true hero.

YOU CAN BE A HERO	Tegla loved running. But more than that, she wanted peace in her country. She helped people run to be friends with each other. Do sports help you get along with others? What can you do to show those around you that peace is important?

ILLUSTRATORS

Talented artists from all over the world brought these heroes to life. We're grateful for their creative powers!

KATHRIN HONESTA	• William Wilberforce, 11 • Jim Henson, 25
LIDIA TOMASHEVSKAYA	• Ralph Lazo, 13 • Marie Curie, 61
EMMA ALLSUP	• Dav Pilkey, 15 • Louis Braille, 29
EDITH KUROSAKA	• Mary Anning, 17 • Caesar Rodney, 53 • Shavarsh Vladimiri Karapetyan, 99
WILIAM LUONG	• Jackie Robinson, 19 • Todd Beamer, 27 • Jamie Oliver, 35 • Sir Edmund Hillary, 37 • Kathrine Switzer, 41 • Jon Huntsman Sr., 51 • Jonas Salk, 55 • César Chávez, 57 • Chris Williams, 59 • Duke Kahanamoku, 63 • Ellen Ochoa, 65 • Fred Rogers, 69 • Frederick Douglass, 71 • "Stagecoach Mary" Fields, 73 • Georg Ferdinand Duckwitz, 75 • Iván Fernández, 77 • Katherine Johnson, 85 • Lin-Manuel Miranda, 87 • Ludwig van Beethoven, 89 • Niels Bohr, 95 • Sarah Emma Edmonds, 97 • Sir Earnest Shackleton, 103 • Gail Halverson, 105 • William Tyndale, 107 • Tegla Loroupe, 109
CHORKUNG KUNG	• Stephen Hawking, 21 • Mohandas Gandhi, 91
SABRINA GENNARI	• Helen Keller, 23
VANYA FIRDAUSYA	• Malala Yousafzai, 31 • Jane Goodall, 39 • J. K. Rowling, 79 • Julia Child, 83
LUCIAGZZ	• Abraham Lincoln, 33 • Harriet Tubman, 101
OLJA MALTZEWA	• J. J. Abrams, 43
SPURGA	• Booker T. Washington, 45
HERUSUOFFICIAL	• John Wooden, 47 • Yasuteru Yamada, 67
VICTORIA	• Corrie ten Boom, 49
ROBERT MILES	• Joshua Chamberlain, 81
ERMIR	• Mother Teresa, 93

ABOUT THE AUTHOR

As a marriage and family therapist, Christy Monson spent years helping clients heal and reframe their lives in Las Vegas and Salt Lake City. She received her BA from Utah State University and an MS from University of Nevada at Las Vegas. The mother of six children and the grandmother to many grandchildren, Christy is now retired and lives in northern Utah. She is the author of several books, including *Love, Hugs, and Hope: When Scary Things Happen* (Familius), *Family Talk* (Familius), and *Becoming Free* (Familius).

BOOK ANGELS

Our deepest gratitude to Michael B., Hallee A., Nancy U., and Nina M., our Book Angels who made 50 *Real Heroes for Boys* possible.